Handbook
OF
Preaching

**And how shall they preach
unless they are sent?**
Romans 10:15

Dr. Nathaniel M. Van Cleave

Foursquare Media

1910 W. Sunset Blvd.
Los Angeles, California 90026
www.foursquaremedia.org

Foursquare Media®
1910 W. Sunset Blvd.
Los Angeles, CA 90026
www.foursquaremedia.org

Contributing Editors:
Larry Libby, Wanda Brackett, and Priscilla Ussery
Project Print Coordinator: Priscilla Ussery
Cover Design and Book Layout: Michelle Glush

ISBN 0-9635581-7-X
Reprint 2007, Foursquare Media®
All rights reserved

Printed in the United States of America

Contents

LaVonna Hopkins
Testimony of her father: Dr. Nathaniel Van Cleave

In 1992, at the age of 85 years, my father was told by his doctor that he had prostate cancer. The doctor suggested that they would like to treat the cancer and see if they could make him more comfortable.

After a long pause, my dad replied, "You know I am a minister and I strongly believe that God can heal our illnesses, even cancer. I also believe the scripture where we are assured that there is an appointed time for man to die. I believe that my life, health and ultimate death are in God's hands. You go ahead and do what you feel is best for me, and I will do as the Scriptures teach and pray that God will have His perfect will in my life."

While Dad was getting dressed, the doctor took my brother Bob aside.

"Bob," he said, "I know your father strongly believes in the power of prayer. I don't want to discourage either of you, but I must tell you that the cancer has spread to the bones. Without God's intervention, I feel he only has about three years left and it will be difficult. Don't share this with him yet. I'll do everything in my power to treat the cancer and keep him comfortable."

When Bob shared these things with me on the phone, we both prayed together and wept, but neither of us told anyone else.

When Dad arrived home that day he called my mother into his study, and together they committed the cancer to God. My mother's faith in God's healing power had always been a source of great strength to our entire family. She never doubted God would heal him and never let a day go by that entire year, that she did not say, "Jesus we claim the victory." Dad spent most of the year in the Word of God, which was his strength.

Dad had just completed writing his commentary on divine healing for the new *Spirit-Filled Life Bible* and had submitted it to the editors. Initially, this caused him some concern. Should his own physical condition be a factor in producing this piece?

Then he prayed: "Oh Father, I have studied your Word from cover to cover many times. Every word I have written in these commentaries is the result of fifty years of careful study on the subject of divine healing. Honor your Word, and your will be done!"

After about one year of treatment, his doctor called him and my brother back to his office.

"Dr. Van Cleave," he began, "my colleagues and I here at the hospital and medical center have reviewed all your tests, numerous times. Last year you had cancer of the prostate in an advanced condition, and now we find no cancer in your body." With tears in his eyes, this unbelieving doctor continued, "Dr. Van Cleave, God had to have healed you of cancer, because we could not!"

My father, Nathaniel Van Cleave went to be with the Lord, December 24, 2002 after 10 more years of fruitful ministry, at the nice old age of 96, cancer free and of sound mind, praising the Lord because it was Christmas!

LaVonna Hopkins
2007

Introduction
My purpose in writing this book...

...is not to add another to the already numerous textbooks of homiletics, many of which are quite complete and excellently written. I am not unaware that I may be motivated partly by a desire for self-expression in my favorite realm of study and teaching. However, I am quite sure that I see a need for a homiletical handbook that can be used conveniently by ministers already in the field in the actual process of sermon preparation. For that reason, this book is arranged so that it follows the steps of preparation in the same order that they are taken in actual sermon construction.

Nearly all textbooks praise the expository sermon, but very few *explain* and *demonstrate* the expository method clearly. In fact, only a few books on preaching give examples to illustrate the different types of sermons and the qualities of organization. In this book, examples will be given in every place where their use will make the explanation clearer.

I will make no attempt within these pages to create a new system of homiletics or to depart from the accepted technical terminology of homiletical science. A handbook is not the place for new contributions to the field, or for striking originality. I have been influenced by, and have obtained ideas from a great many books, many of which will be listed at the end of these chapters, so that any who desire to research in the field may be helped to good sources.

I make this contribution with a prayer that it may help to lift the general level of preaching ability.

N. M. Van Cleave

Preaching is not merely human discourse...

True gospel preaching is a channel through which divine grace flows to human hearts. The gospel preacher becomes a vessel by which God mediates redemption and healing. Preaching is not merely a chosen activity of men. Preachers and teachers are placed in the Church by God; they are special members in the Body of Christ (Ephesians 4:11). Consequently, their preaching is influenced by the working of the Holy Spirit, who abides in the Church. Mark concludes his Gospel with these words, "And they went out and preached everywhere, the Lord working with them and confirming *the Word* through the accompanying signs" (NKJV).

The Spirit empowers the preacher, opens the hearts of the hearers, and confirms the message of the Word.

When the Word of God is preached, three entities are involved: the preacher, the hearers, and the Holy Spirit. The Spirit empowers the preacher, opens the hearts of the hearers, and confirms the message of the Word so that there is true communication. But the communication does not flow only in one direction; the Spirit effects a feedback response to the minister, creating a two-directional flow and resulting in an act of worship.

Preaching is a true part of the church's worship. In fact, it may be the crowning event in the worship service. Perhaps that is why Paul urged upon the Ephesian church their continual prayers for him that his preaching would have a true charisma: "Praying always with all prayer and supplication in the Spirit....and for me, that utterance may be given to me, that I may open my mouth boldly to make known the mystery of the gospel, for which I am an ambassador in chains; that in it I may speak *boldly* as I ought to speak" (Ephesians 6:18-20, NKJV).

The Greek word translated "boldly" is the same word used in Acts 4:31, "And when they had prayed, the place was shaken where they assembled together, and they were filled with the Holy Spirit and they spoke the word of God with *boldness.*" To the Apostles, that kind of anointed speaking and preaching was without a doubt the crowning event in the act of worship. Some today believe that the sermon is something added on to, or following the worship service. Everything in the service, the songs, the prayers, the gifted utterance, should prepare hearts for the preaching of the Word, all of which together constitute the complete act of worship.

Homiletics... helps us to skillfully handle the Word of truth and to present it in the most effective manner.

A careful study of the Word will bear out the fact that, while preaching is a Spirit-empowered exercise employed by God to communicate divine truth, it also requires human effort in study and preparation. Preaching has a divine element and a human element. It may well be that the human element is very small compared with the divine element, but I feel certain that, however small our human part in preaching may be, we should perform that human part with all the diligence and care possible to us.

"Be diligent to present yourself approved to God, a worker who does not need to be ashamed, rightly dividing the Word of truth." — *2 Timothy 2:15*

Homiletics has to do with the human part of preaching. It helps us to skillfully handle the Word of truth and to present it in the most effective manner. If, however, prayer and dedication are missing from our preparation, the sermon will lack charisma and will contribute little to worship. The apostle Paul speaks clearly of the balance of the human and divine aspects of ministry.

A preacher who aims at nothing is sure to hit it. Choose a target and then take careful aim.

These things command and teach.

Let no one despise your youth, but be an example to the believers in word, in conduct, in love, in spirit, in faith, in purity. Till I come, give attention to reading, to exhortation, to doctrine. Do not neglect the gift that is in you, which was given to you by prophecy with the laying on of the hands of the eldership. Meditate on these things; give yourself entirely to them, that your progress may be evident to all. Take heed to yourself and to the doctrine. Continue in them, for in doing this you will save both yourself and those who hear you.

— *1 Timothy 4:11-16*

Chapter One

Selecting a Theme

A sermon needs a theme...

...for the same reason that a building needs a blueprint or a story needs a plot. Yet it is a lamentable fact that many sermons lack a clear theme that can be intelligently followed. A sermon without a strong theme is like a flood that spreads in *every direction*; a sermon with a theme is like a river flowing within its banks in a *certain direction*. Rivers are of great value to man; floods are spectacular, but seldom of any value.

A sermon is not a thing merely to be displayed; it is a means to an end. A preacher must first determine the goal to be reached before taking the first step in preparation. A good hunter does not fire in all directions, hoping to hit something. He first sights his game and then takes aim. A preacher who aims at nothing is sure to hit it. Choose a target and then take careful aim. The choice of a worthy theme is a very large step toward successful sermon construction.

The first question good preachers ask is, "What do my people need at this time?"

The theme must not be confused with a subject or topic. A topic should accurately suggest the theme, but the theme is nearly always longer and more complete than the topic. The topic is for the bulletin board or newspaper; the theme is the preacher's own statement of the purpose of the sermon. The topic is announced at the beginning before the text is read or immediately afterward; the theme is stated more fully somewhere in the introduction. For that matter, the theme need not be stated at all if the divisions make it sufficiently clear, in which case it serves simply to guide the preacher in making divisions.

In 2 Timothy 4:6-8, for example, we might state the theme like this: *"The significance that Paul's last message has to every Christian."*

PAUL'S SWAN SONG
Text: 2 Timothy 4:6-8
I.   Its Significance in Life's Battles:
     "I have fought a good fight."
II. Its Significance in Life's Race:
     "I have finished my course."
III. Its Significance in Life's Doubts:
     "I have kept the faith."
IV. Its Significance at Life's End:
     "There is laid up for me a crown."

That the words of Paul have significance for all Christians is seen in the phrase, "and not to me only, but unto all them also who love His appearing."

There are, generally speaking, two kinds of themes in regard to grammatical structure: the rhetorical and the logical. These terms are used with a specific technical meaning.

A rhetorical theme or proposition is a subject with its modifiers, such as "The Blessings of God's People," or "The Perils of Life's Journey," or "The Sinner's Need of Repentance." Single words such as "Repentance" or "Faith" are too general for themes; they need modifiers such as adjectives or prepositional phrases to make them sufficiently specific for themes.

A logical theme consists of a subject and a predicate, such as "Faith in Christ is the only means to salvation," or "Happiness is not found in possessions only." The logical theme may be in question form: "Why is faith in Christ necessary to salvation?" The logical theme suggests divisions that are proofs of the theme; or in the question form, the divisions are answers to the question. Note that the above themes have a verb as well as a subject.

The important thing is to select the proper theme for the occasion. The first question good preachers ask is, "What do my people need at this time?" The first question should not be, "Where can I find a clever outline?" A doctor does not give all his patients the same medicine, nor does he give medicine at all without a diagnosis, unless he is a quack. A preacher who preaches sermons without diagnosing the people's needs is a ministerial quack, and will do people about as much good as a quack doctor.

People's needs are discovered several ways. They may be revealed to the preacher in prayer, for many needs are secret needs. Visitation in the people's homes will usually solve the problem of what to preach, for during such visits, people often voice their needs and make confessions of their weaknesses if the preacher is a sympathetic hearer. Frequently some general condition in the community such as an epidemic of sickness, a calamity, or a general moral trend will suggest the proper theme.

Preachers must use every opportunity to quote, teach, and honor the Scriptures.

The special holidays of the year usually call for a related theme for one of the services, but, of course, the sermons should always be built upon an appropriate Bible truth. For instance, near the Fourth of July the theme might be, "The Believer's Declaration of Independence." Near Thanksgiving the theme might be, "In Everything Give Thanks."

Evangelists or special speakers will find it more difficult to discern people's needs than the pastor although the pastor may help them. But, by all means, evangelists ought to pray definitely about the choice of the theme. Where they repeat sermons, they should, after prayer and diagnosis, revise them to fit the present situation and people.

A sermon theme should be comprehensive, biblical, dynamic and specific.

- The theme should express the whole aim of the sermon, nothing more or less.
- A good theme is biblical; otherwise its elaboration could hardly be called a sermon. Secular themes may be chosen, but they should be rare.
- A proper theme is dynamic. It starts the hearers thinking in a certain direction. The theme that does not arouse interest and stir mental activity is not the right one for the occasion.
- Finally, a theme ought to be specific. People are not intensely interested in the general subject of "Faith," but many are interested in "Faith that Overcomes the World," or "Faith that Obtains Salvation."

When a proper theme has been selected, the preacher is ready to proceed to the next step.

Chapter Two

Choosing and Interpreting a Text

Since the gospel is found only in the Bible...

...which is God's inspired revelation, a sermon ought to be based on Scripture. It is important that people know the Bible thoroughly, and preachers must use every opportunity to quote, teach, and honor the Scriptures.

The selection of a text will depend upon a preacher's approach to the sermon. If the theme is chosen first, then the text must be selected that will best support the theme without distorting or accommodating the text. This can be done by tracing in a concordance the words that are synonymous to the principal word in the theme and then by applying the process of elimination. Or a satisfactory text that harmonizes with the theme may be revealed to the preacher, with a little meditation or prayer.

Preachers need not fear that they will be thought naïve or inexperienced because they use a familiar text; the great preachers of every age have used these great texts.

When a theme is chosen first, its exact wording should await the selection of a text so that the theme and text may be harmonized. For instance, a preacher may feel that the present need is for personal evangelism and tentatively words the theme, "Our Responsibility in Personal Evangelism."

Selecting John 1:40-51 as a text, concerning Andrew and Philip finding Peter and Nathaniel, the preacher may revise the theme to read, "The Example of the First Disciples in Personal Evangelism." This outline might follow:

    I.   They personally learned about Jesus.
    II. They preached Jesus to another.
    III. They invited another to meet Jesus.

If the preacher wants to follow with another sermon on the best methods of personal evangelism, the tentative theme may be, "How to Become a Successful Personal Evangelist."

After selecting the text in Acts 8 about Philip and the Eunuch, the preacher revises the theme to read, "A Successful Revivalist Shows the Way to Personal Evangelism." This outline might result:

    I.   The guide is the Holy Spirit.
    II.   The starting point is the prospect's interest.
    III. The approach is through the Scripture.
    IV. The subject is Christ.
    V.   The aim is a full surrender.

Quite frequently, and this is the ideal, the text will be chosen before the theme while the preacher is praying or studying the Bible. But when the need of the people gives rise to the sermon, a theme will often be developed first. However, if the preacher's mind is saturated with Scripture and people's problems are viewed in the light of biblical solutions, a text is easily suggested, even as a physician thinks of sickness in the terms of specific remedies and specific kinds of operations. If the preacher is following a series sermons through a particular book of the Bible, of course, the text will come before the theme, though there will be a general theme for the whole book chosen at the beginning of the series.

We are concerned in this chapter with the selection of a text. The following guidelines are suggested:

1. Select a real text. A real text is one that is a complete statement, precept, or narrative used with the sense intended by the author. Single words or fragment texts are to be avoided. Any legitimate theme can be based on a real text. Texts that are isolated from the context and accommodated to an application foreign to the purpose of the author are not proper texts. "Let us do evil that good may come" is a sentence from the Bible. But when it is isolated from the context, it is contrary to the teaching of the sacred author and, as such, is inappropriate as a scriptural text.

It is not good taste to quote Greek and Hebrew in the pulpit, for hardly anyone in the average congregation will appreciate the quotations. Give people the benefits of thorough research, but do not display methods.

2. Select the great doctrinal and ethical texts of the Bible. Do not fear that these have been exhausted because they are used frequently. They are used frequently because they are great preaching texts. Preachers need not fear that they will be thought naïve or inexperienced because they use a familiar text; the great preachers of every age have used these great texts. People are interested in them because they have used them for comfort and light in dark places.

3. Avoid texts known to be interpolations. Interpolations are portions that have crept into the later manuscripts through scribes' errors or additions from marginal notes, and are not found in the oldest and most reliable manuscripts. These spurious texts can be avoided by using a reliable translation for comparison in study. These texts are not numerous, and none of them contain false teaching, but many educated hearers know of them and a sermon based on a spurious text would have no authority with them.

4. Avoid the sayings of uninspired men when choosing a text. These sayings have their place in the Bible, but they are not proper texts. Many preachers have selected texts from the words of Job's friends in the book of Job. Some of these sound good when isolated, but all three of the speakers were in error and were rebuked by God. The words of Pharaoh, Satan, Balaam, Pilate, and any other men are recorded, but these people were not inspired apostles or prophets.

5. Do not choose texts simply because they are odd or unusual. Serious preachers have no time for novelties and curiosities. Humor is not forbidden in the pulpit when it is in good taste, but preachers should not be funny at the expense of the Holy Word. Texts that seem strange appear so only because they are oriental or old English idioms. A preacher once selected the text from Hosea, "Ephraim is a cake not turned," with the topic, "Half Baked." The only thing "half baked" in the modern sense of the term was the sermon.

Before a text can be expressed in an intelligent theme and divided, it must be properly interpreted. Observe the following rules of interpretation:

1. Interpret the text in the light of the context. A verse of Scripture that seems to have one meaning may be seen to mean something else when the context is read. First Corinthians 2:9 seems to refer to heaven's future glory, but the context reveals it to be a quotation from the Old Testament predicting the fuller revelations of the age of grace that believers may enjoy in this present world. Hebrews 12:1 appears to be an admonition to believers to live carefully before their unsaved neighbors, but the context (chapter 11) shows that it refers to the believer's race as encompassed about by the great heroes of faith (the great cloud of martyrs of chapter 11). Colossians 2:21, "Touch not, taste not, handle not," seems to be a good prohibition text, but it is useless as such because it is a quotation of some negative precepts that legalistic teachers were using. Texts such as the above are numerous, and interpreting them is never safe until the context has been studied.

No one admires chaos, nor can hearers be expected to listen attentively to chaotic sermons.

2. Interpret a text in harmony with the teaching of the whole Bible. The Bible does not contradict itself. Therefore, when the text can have two meanings, the one is to be taken is the one that is in harmony with the teaching of the body of Scripture. Luke 14:26 seems to assert that a disciple of Jesus must hate his near relatives, but this would be contrary to the body of Scripture that teaches love, so the word "hate" must be taken figuratively as hyperbole. This verse really means that a disciple must be willing to give up home ties to heed the call to service.

3. The text must be interpreted in harmony with sound, systematic doctrine. Doctrines are formed after consulting the whole Bible's teaching on a subject. A single text that seems contrary must not be used against the well established Bible doctrine. The orthodox tenets of the fundamental church have been subject to two millennia of scholarly interpretation. This does not guarantee their infallibility, but people should proceed with great caution when interpreting a text contrary to the general fundamental consensus of opinion.

4. A text should be taken literally unless it is obviously figurative or unless a literal interpretation would lead to an absurdity or impossibility. The Bible was written in the common people's language and for average readers. Unrestricted spiritualizing and allegorizing corrupts and compromises the intended meaning of the Bible and makes it little more than a playground for metaphysical minds. That spiritualizing is unproductive is seen by the fact that no two such interpreters get the same result. There are certainly figures of speech in the Bible, but they are, in nearly every case, so obvious that there should be no confusion. In nearly every case where a Bible narrative is allegorized, the forced application is inferior to the real and literal application.

5. If possible, consult the original languages as a help to interpretation. But first a few lines of caution are needed. Preachers should not try to make independent translations of words or passages of the Greek and Hebrew texts unless they have studied the grammar of these languages. Some preachers quote the original words from hearsay, trusting the accuracy of another's research. This practice has led to some absurd renderings of Greek passages that have been traced through several people, all of whom quoted from hearsay. Furthermore, it is not good taste to quote Greek and Hebrew in the pulpit, for hardly anyone in the average congregation will appreciate the quotations. Give people the benefits of thorough research, but do not display methods. Everyone knows that an artist uses a brush to paint his pictures, but we do not expect to see brush marks on the finished painting. These warnings

A sermon has permanent value only if it can be remembered.

need not discourage Greek students; they can profit immeasurably by their studies. There are literally scores of passages, the full depth of which cannot be seen in any English translation. There are also a number of homiletical hints that are discovered in the study of the original languages.

6. Preachers who do not have a thorough knowledge of the original languages will be helped to interpret the text by comparing several different translations of the Bible. It will be found helpful to use three types of versions in textual study:

- A reliable translation, such as *The New King James Version*
- A literal translation, such as *Young's Literal Translation, Rotherham's Emphasized Bible*, or *Marshal's Interlinear Greek and English New Testament*
- A paraphrase, such as *The Living Bible, The Amplified Bible; The New Testament: An Expanded Translation*, by Kenneth S. Wuest; or *The New Testament in Modern English*, by J. B. Phillips

By comparing textual reading in several versions, people can avoid misinterpretations based upon archaic words.

Much help may be obtained from the use of an analytical concordance, such as Young's or Strong's. Many pastors who have not studied the original languages find great help in the use of word-books such as *Vine's Expository Dictionary of New Testament Words* and *Wilson's Old Testament Word Studies*.

A sermon that does not have unity is not truly a sermon, but several little talks strung together.

7. **Consult parallel passages.** Scripture is best interpreted by Scripture. If the same idea is expressed several places, but in somewhat different words, it is made clear by comparison. If an ethical principle is applied to several different cases, it is seen to be general in application and not simply a local emergency measure. Some commands and prohibitions are of only local and temporary significance, and others are meant for the whole church for all time. This problem of application can usually be solved by comparing parallel passages.

8. **Consult a good critical, exegetical commentary.** Devotional commentaries seldom give much attention to interpretation, although they are helpful in suggesting points for elaboration. But here we are interested only in the interpretation of the text, which must come before elaboration. The writers of the good exegetical commentaries were careful Biblical scholars conversant with theology and the original languages, and, while they are not infallible, of course, their opinions are worth considering. Preachers should not be slavish followers of commentaries, nor should they reject their explanations without good reason and careful study.

Chapter Three

Organizing Your Sermon

Stones, wool, steel, and glass do not make a building...

Paints, easel, and brushes do not make a painting. Stone, hammer, and chisels do not make a statue. Steel, glass, rubber, and cotton do not make an automobile. Likewise, facts, illustrations, proofs, and application do not make a sermon; the only difference in each case between the materials and the finished product is *organization*. Following are some of the reasons for organization in the sermon:

1. **Organization facilitates the delivery.** It is easier to remember the sermon thoughts if they are arranged so that logically related thoughts follow one another. It is easier to keep the whole body of material in mind if it has a plan. An untrained preacher may suppose that he has more liberty of delivery if he is free to say whatever comes to his mind on any subject, but such talk would have to be labeled, "miscellaneous thoughts on religion." A preacher will find that the organized discourse is easier to deliver; furthermore, what he delivers will deserve the name "sermon."

> *Listening to a sermon is like riding a bicycle; when the progress stops, you fall off.*

27

2. An organized sermon is more pleasing to the hearers and has more beauty. If some object that preachers should not strive for beauty in preaching, we answer, "Why not?" Jesus on the mount preached the most beautiful sermon of all and it was certainly well organized. We precede our sermons with beautiful music to make the service more attractive, so why should the sermon lack attractiveness? No one admires chaos, nor can hearers be expected to listen attentively to chaotic sermons. Sensational stories, humor, and pulpit antics will not make up for poorly planned material.

Progress is hindered by digressions from the theme. Side trips do not take you nearer home.

3. An organized sermon is easier to remember. A sermon has permanent value only if it can be remembered. People do not face their problems during the service hours on Sunday, but during the week when at work, while transacting business, or in the company of unbelievers. Their ability to solve problems as they arise depends upon their ability to call to mind admonitions and counsel given by the pastor in church. If they fail in the time of trial, the pastor who cares only for temporary impressions is, to some degree, responsible. Now, of course, we strive to get immediate results from preaching, but we should strive just as much for permanent results. Consider the outline by Alexander McClaren below, which is developed from a well known text.

Text: John 3:16
I.   The Great Lake — God So Loved the World
II. The River —That He Gave His Son

III. The Pitcher — Whosoever Believeth on Him

IV. The Drink — Should Have Everlasting Life

The outline creates a picture of a lake, out of which flows a river, into which a pitcher is dipped, and from which a drink is taken. People can easily grasp and retain concepts presented in such a way. Every time afterward that they see a lake, river or pitcher, the sermon is likely to come to mind.

4. An organized sermon can be easily understood. A well organized sermon will seldom be vague, for organization dispels ambiguity. One of the best ways to determine whether people really understand a subject is to attempt to organize the subject. Educators know that no body of truth can be transferred from one person to another in bulk. The parts must be imparted one by one in systematic order. A sermon is a short course of instruction on a specific subject, followed by an appeal. The lessons must be separated and given one at a time in their logical order if the hearers are to clearly understand the contents and purpose of the sermon.

A sermon must not only move but must finally reach an adequate goal.

5. Finally, organization increases the effectiveness of a sermon. Preachers can learn this lesson from salesmen and lawyers. Salesmen know how to approach clients and just when to make their appeal. They stay on the subject and present the merits of their products one by one until the buyers have a mental picture of themselves as the delighted owners of the products. Lawyers carefully build an appeal for their clients step by step until juries cannot picture them other than innocent. An unorganized appeal would be just so much talk that would fall on deaf ears. Now it is not being overlooked that the Holy Spirit is the largest power in the sermon's effectiveness. Preachers must pray over their sermons and commit them to God; but if people have any part in the sermons, they should make their part as effective as possible. Doing the human part poorly does not make the divine part more effective.

Now that we have seen the advantages of organization, let us look further to the *qualities* that the organization should exhibit. Consider the following:

1. First and foremost, the sermon should have unity. By unity, we mean that one theme prevails through all the divisions. Each division is related to the theme, and there is something common to each division. In other words, there is a "common denominator," for, when a sermon has unity, some common idea will go into each division. A sermon that does not have unity is not truly a sermon, but several little talks strung together. Preachers cannot expect to be sufficiently forceful to alter people's conduct in a thirty-minute sermon unless they stay on one idea or duty. The prayerless are not going to be turned to a prayerful life by hearing several remarks about prayer in a sermon, along with a good many other assorted ideas. On the other hand, if preachers devote a whole half hour to enforcing prayer as Christian duty, they are likely to get some

A topical sermon is more likely than other type of sermon to be shaped by the preacher's personal views and prejudices.

results. Preachers may find, in fact, that they need to preach a series of sermons on prayer before they see real results. If a carpenter wants to drive a nail, he must pound in one place. The following illustrates unity:

TOPIC: THE THRONE OF GRACE
Text: Hebrews 4:16
Theme: Approaching the Throne of Grace
I.   How **We Approach the Throne of Grace:** "With boldness"
II. Why **We Approach the Throne of Grace:** "To obtain mercy and receive help"
III. When **We Approach the Throne of Grace:** "In the time of need" — at all times

Notice that something is common to each division and that the theme follows throughout. To introduce an appeal for tithing into the above outline would violate the unity. If people need to hear about tithing, devote a whole sermon to it.

2. The sermon should have coherence. The parts must be related to a common theme, and they should adhere to one another. The following outline has unity but not much coherence.

I.   God is the author of faith.
II. Without faith a Christian will fail.
III. Faith is necessary to salvation.

Faith is common to all the above divisions, but the divisions have little relation to one another. The following outline has both unity and coherence.

TOPIC: PAUL'S THREE I AM'S
Text: Romans 1:14-16
Theme: Paul's state of mind regarding the preaching of the Gospel of Christ
I.   I am a debtor **to preach,** v.14.
II. I am not ashamed **to preach,** v. 16.
III. I am ready **to preach,** v. 15.

Very important to coherence is smooth transition from one point to the next. This may be accomplished by transitional phrases that unite divisions I and II by saying, "Paul not only voiced a feeling of indebtedness to preach the gospel in Rome but also made it clear that he was not ashamed to do so." The divisions of a sermon must not be a series of little "sermonettes" loosely strung together. Each division must be logically related and arranged so that each is a logical step upward toward the goal or climax.

3. The sermon should have steady progress. This quality assures that the hearers will be carried along to the goal. Listening to a sermon is like riding a bicycle; when the progress stops, you fall off. Progress is achieved by arranging the divisions so that each rises a little nearer to the goal. Progress is hindered by digressions from the theme. Side trips do not take you nearer home. Progress is further hindered by too much needless elaboration of a single division. If there are only two or three main divisions, there should be several subdivisions under each to keep the discourse moving. Preachers can help make the progress apparent by announcing their goals and the main mile posts at the beginning. The following outline illustrates progress:

Text: Mark 1:14-15
I.   Jesus came – His advent.
II. Jesus came preaching – His mission.
III. Jesus came preaching repentance – His message.

Note that each division rises a little above the preceding one, reaching a climax. Such an outline properly handled would be sure to sustain interest because it progresses.

4. The sermon should have symmetry. Symmetry or proportion is necessary to all works of art. A house with a porch as big as the building would be both odd and impractical. However, sermons frequently lack symmetry. Too much time may be spent in the introduction and in the first points, causing the latter divisions to be slighted. Sometimes a subdivision is enlarged far out of proportion to its importance, so that both symmetry and progress are violated. If the subdivision were that important, another should have been chosen, and the subdivision should have been made a main division.

Nearly all human problems are treated in the Scriptures, if not specifically, at least in principle.

It is not necessary that all divisions be of equal length, but time should be devoted to each in proportion to its importance. If all the divisions are of equal importance, then each should receive the same treatment, but this is seldom a fact. Symmetry cannot be demonstrated with an outline because it is achieved very largely in the delivery.

5. Finally, the sermon should have a climax. The older meaning of the word "climax" is the same as progress. It is from a Greek word that means "ladder." The word, however, has come to mean the final highest point of development. A sermon may have progress, but it may not leave the impression that a goal has been reached. A sermon may steadily rise, yet fail to arrive at any point that could be called a proper goal. Therefore, a sermon must not only move but must finally reach an adequate goal, as indicated by the theme. An arrow shot into the air makes progress upward, but it does not reach a goal; it falls to the ground when its momentum stops. An arrow shot at a target hits the mark. It then has both progress and climax, and the archer is satisfied. Climax in a sermon is achieved in the *construction* by arranging the points so that a goal is reached at the end of the sermon. Climax is achieved in the *delivery* by starting in a deliberate but unimpassioned voice, and then gradually increasing the emphasis and gestures as the sermon progresses so that the most intense point is at the appeal. Note the following illustration of climax:

Texts need not be accommodated, for the real application is nearly always richer than one that is forced.

TOPIC: CHRISTIAN ATTAINMENT
Text: Philippians 3:13-15
Theme: The Christian's Attitude toward Attainment
I. His Attitude toward Past Attainment —
   Humble forgetfulness

II. His Attitude toward Present Attainment —
    Earnest reaching forth

III. His Attitude toward Future Attainment —
    Confident expectation of perfection

Though the above is not a perfect sermon, it does reach a goal to which nothing can be added. It has a climax.

Let us recapitulate. The qualities of good sermon organization are unity, coherence, progress, symmetry, and climax.

Chapter Four

Types of Sermons and Their Functions

We have seen how to select a theme...

...how to choose and interpret a text, and how to organize a sermon. Let us now see what kinds of sermons there are and what the function of each kind is. Not all authorities classify sermons in the same way, but sermons are most commonly classified as (1) Topical, (2) Textual, and (3) Expository. We will follow this classification that is based upon the *use* made of the *text* in the construction of the sermon:

1. The topical sermon takes from the text only a topic or subject. The divisions are invented by the preacher in accordance with the rhetorical possibilities of the subject and the preacher's knowledge of the subject as it is treated in the whole Bible. Consider the following examples:

REDEMPTION
I. The Meaning of Redemption
II. The Necessity of Redemption
III. The Method of Redemption
IV. The Results of Redemption

EVIDENCES OF GOD'S LOVE
I.   As Seen in the Bible
II. As Seen in Nature
III. As Seen in Providence

The topical method permits full liberty of composition and full treatment of any subject, gives unlimited rein to a preacher's inventive genius, and opens a wide door to rhetorical eloquence. However, a topical sermon is more likely than other type of sermon to be shaped by the preacher's personal views and prejudices. It can also be too general in its scope and may be too secular in content. Another objection to the topical method is that the divisions are like links in a chain instead of parts of a designed structure; the number of the chain divisions is arbitrary, and in most cases there could be more or fewer divisions without doing serious damage to the sermon. For instance, in the second example given above, there is no good reason, except limitation of time, that other "Evidence of God's Love" might not be included.

If preachers have any dramatic ability whatever, they can make the Bible scenes and Bible people alive again in a fascinating manner.

Though the disadvantages seem to outweigh the advantages of topical preaching, there are times that the topical method is preferred. Topical sermons are recommended in the following circumstances:

- When the subject is not adequately treated by any passage of Scripture
- When a preacher desires to treat a subject in a very

general way, such as presenting a doctrine to an audience to which it is entirely unfamiliar

- When a preacher desires to present general evangelistic truth to an audience of unsaved people who are not familiar with the Bible
- When treating social or moral problems not existing in Bible times or not treated by Bible writers

2. The textual sermon takes from the text a subject and the main divisions. The main points of the sermon are stated or clearly inferred by the passage of Scripture upon which the sermon is based. However, the subdivisions are invented in the same way that all the divisions are invented in the topical sermon. Consider the following:

THE MINISTER, AN EXAMPLE
Text: 1 Timothy 4:12
"Become an example of believers in word, in conduct, in love, in purity" (Revised Version).
I. An Example in Word
II. An Example in Conduct
III. An Example in Love
IV. An Example in Faith
V. An Example in Purity

The text simply mentions the exemplary qualities of word, conduct, love, faith, and purity; no more information is available without drawing upon several other parts of the Bible or upon personal experience. The sermon is textual because the text provides the main divisions, while the subdivisions or the elaboration is drawn from other sources

Textual sermons have the advantage of being more

scriptural in design than the topical variety. They do not disappoint hearers who expect something from the text. The textual method permits great variety in construction and selection. The textual sermon seems more like a finished discourse because the number of divisions is determined by the material in the text, and when each division has been treated, no one expects anything more. In most cases, a textual sermon will be remembered longer, for if the hearers follow the sermon in their Bibles, a connection is made between the passage and the preacher's admonitions so that the message is easily recalled every time the passage is read.

Some object that the textual method restricts a preacher's originality, but this is not necessarily true; that it does not permit a sufficiently broad treatment of a subject, but most sermons are too broad; and that textual preachers too often accommodate their texts and corrupt or compromise the true meaning. The last objection is a real one, but texts need not be accommodated, for the real application is nearly always richer than one that is forced. The reason some preachers accommodate their texts is that they are following an outmoded practice that was followed for several generations in Europe and America from which period a great many printed sermons have been borrowed. Very few of the better preachers today who are well trained and who accept the Bible as the divine revelation are guilty of purposely forcing their texts.

Expository preaching restrains any tendency to ride a hobbyhorse or to preach only pet doctrines.

Textual sermons are recommended in the following circumstances:

- When a single passage of Scripture will provide the principal points to meet the needs of the hearers
- When preaching ethical sermons, because a text carries more authority for preaching specific evangelistic truth
- When dealing with specific doctrinal truths

3. The expository sermon takes from the text not only a subject and main divisions but also all the subdivisions. It is usually based on a longer passage than the topical or textual sermon. Often the text is a whole paragraph, whole chapter, or even a whole book. No idea can be introduced into the expository sermon that does not come from the passage of Scripture upon which it is based. It is an exposition of the given passage and that only. Note the following example:

TEMPTATION

Text: James 1:12-15

I. The Origin of Temptation, vv. 13-14
    A, Not from God, v.13
    B. From inward desire, v.14

II. The Results of Yielding to Temptation, v. 15
    A. First sin, v.15
    B. Then death, v.15

III. The Reward of Enduring Temptation, v.12
    A. Blessedness, v.12
    B. A crown of life, v.12

The text of the above example consists of four verses, a complete paragraph. Every heading and subheading is taken from the passage of Scripture used for the text.

Expository preaching, I believe, has many more note-worthy advantages:

- It is most like the preaching of the Apostles and early preachers.
- It leads both the preacher and the hearers to a wider and deeper knowledge of the Scripture.
- It promotes a greater respect for the Bible on the part of the laity.
- It restrains the tendency to loose interpretation and accommodation.
- It restrains any tendency to ride a hobbyhorse or to preach only pet doctrines.
- It prevents voice monotony in preaching in that the variety of material is likely to demand flexibility in volume and pitch.
- Where exposition is used in a series, it makes easier the choice of a text.
- It makes easier the introduction of unwelcome admonitions, and the preacher is less likely to be accused of preaching to individuals; if the offensive injunction falls within the text, no one can blame the preacher for making several remarks about it.

Several objections to the expository method of preaching are commonly made. Some object that it is not conducive to unity in the sermon. But expository sermons can and should have unity like other types. Some contend that it is not adaptable to meeting up-to-date problems. Nearly all human problems are treated in the Scriptures, if not specifically, at least in principle. Good expository preachers are no less interested in application than others. It is further objected that it is not sufficiently sensa-

Scripture is very frequently explained by Scripture.

tional for modern times. Certainly the Bible equals any source for human interest and mighty deeds. If preachers have any dramatic ability whatever, they can make the Bible scenes and Bible people alive again in a fascinating manner. Furthermore, preachers should not be interested in sensation for sensation's sake; cheap journalistic preaching sows only in shallow and thorny soil. It gets quick results, but not lasting results. Most of the objectors to expository preaching either do not understand the method, or the expository sermons they have heard have been poor examples. Expository preaching is often confused with a running commentary of the Sunday School lesson variety, or the exegetical Bible lecture. The true expository sermon has organization, a goal, and a climax like any other sermon.

Analysis is like classifying the strata of marble in a quarry; synthesis is building a structure out of that same marble.

Expository preaching is recommended in the following cases:

- When the need of the occasion can be met with a consecutive passage containing all the points necessary to the need
- When preaching a series or course of sermons
- When treating a narrative, parable, or psalm
- When dealing with a passage longer than one or two verses
- When preaching on a book of the Bible
- When preaching on Bible characters where the material is not too far scattered
- When preaching on great chapters of the Bible

- Evangelistic preaching when the sermon is based on a story, parable, or incident

We have studied the theme, the text, the sermon organization and the sermon classifications with their uses. We have selected a theme and a text. We know what qualities the organization must have, and we have selected the type of sermon that is best for the occasion. We will now see how to construct the sermon; first, the topical sermon, then the textual, and, finally, the expository sermon.

Chapter Five
Constructing a Topical Sermon
The ways of constructing a topical sermon...

...might be multiplied indefinitely, depending upon one's ability to distinguish minute variations. For the sake of convenience in classification, we will list five: (1) by aspect; (2) by proofs; (3) by illustrations; (4) by order of materials; (5) by analogy. Consider the following guidelines:

1. **A topical sermon may be composed by displaying its aspects.** This may be approached in two ways: by simply noting the aspects, or by asking questions that will bring out the aspects. By aspect, we mean point of view, or way of looking at a subject. Three examples follow:

To analyze a text is simply to separate its parts so as to note and examine them separately.

PRAYER
Its Meaning
I. Its Necessity
II. Its Method
III. Its Results

FAITH
I.   What is faith?
II. Why is it needed?
III. How is it received?
IV. What will it accomplish?

THE GOSPEL
I.   The Origin of the Gospel
II. The Purpose of the Gospel
III. The Power of the Gospel

2. A topical sermon may be constructed also by stating its proofs. This method is best for controversial themes or where the theme is a statement of fact (a logical theme). Note the examples below:

THE RESURRECTION OF CHRIST
The Argument of Faith — The Bible declares it.
I.   The Argument from Testimony — There are many competent witnesses.
II. The Argument from History — The Church is successful.

CHRIST, THE MESSIAH
I.   Proof from Old Testament Prophecy
II. Proof from Christ's Works
III. Proof from Christ's Claims
IV. Proof from the Powers of His Gospel

3. A topical sermon may be developed by advancing illustrations of the theme taken from Bible incidents and biographies or even by illustration from church history. Consider these two examples:

The Disciplinary Values of Delay
I. As seen in the case of Moses
II. As seen in the case of Elijah
III. As seen in the case of Paul

The Influence of a Godly Mother
I. Observed in Moses
II. Observed in Samuel
III. Observed in Timothy

In the outline above such later men as St. Augustine and John Wesley might be used in addition to Bible characters.

4. A topical sermon may be developed according to the kinds of material used in a sermon: explanation, argument, illustration, and application. This is not a very high order of construction, but it is convenient when there is time only for hasty preparation, and it is better than wandering aimlessly. Something like this method is used often by public speakers for short speeches or sales talks. An example follows:

Christian Tithing
I. Explain it — State what it means.
I. Prove it — Quote Scriptures.
I. Illustrate it — Give examples of benefited tithers.
I. Apply it — Urge hearers to adapt it.

5. Finally, a topical sermon may be developed by treating a subject part by part or step by step, when such a treatment can be given spiritual significance. Note the following examples:

HUSBANDRY OF THE CHRISTIAN LIFE
I. The Sowing — Working for God
II. The Cultivating — Prayer, Bible Study
III. The Reaping — Blessing, Life Eternal

THE COURTROOM OF LIFE
I. The Judge — God, the Father
II. The Accuser — Satan
III. The Advocate — Jesus
IV. The Verdict — Not Guilty

An almost unlimited number of sermon analogies can be used, and analogical form is one of the most attractive forms for a topical sermon.

Chapter Six

Constructing a Textual Sermon

A textual sermon draws its main divisions from the text.

Clearly, this requires a different technique from that of making topical divisions. Here the subject is not divided to suit the preacher's fancy, but as the text indicates or permits by the scope of its material. The textual sermon differs from the expository sermon in that the textual sermon derives from the text only a skeleton that is completed in any way that the preacher desires or that the subject requires, while the expository sermon derives from the text both the skeleton and flesh.

For the sake of convenience, two methods of making textual divisions will be considered. The first method is *analysis;* the second is *synthesis.* Explanations follow:

If the text order is not the logical order for discourse, the order may be changed to suit the purpose of the sermon.

1. **Analysis, or "taking apart," involves an explanation of the parts of a particular text, along with their relationships to one another.** The ideas, duties, doctrines, arguments, classifications, conditions, doctrines, questions, or admonitions of the text would be considered in the order in

which they appear in the text. Some people think that analysis is the easiest and most natural way of dividing a text, since it requires only the ability to discover the parts and to find relationships. This type of treatment should not be used, however, where no unity exits between the parts or where the order of the parts is not suitable for the purpose of the sermon. Observe the following examples:

THE CHRISTIAN EXAMPLE

1 Timothy 4:12 (Related Admonitions)

"Be an example to the believers in word, in conduct, in love, in spirit, in faith, in purity."

I.   An Example in Word
II. An Example in Conduct
III. An Example in Love
IV. An Example in Spirit
V.   An Example in Faith
VI. An Example in Purity

THREE DUTIES OF A YOUNG MINISTER

1 Timothy 4:13 (Related Duties)

I.   Reading
II. Exhorting
III. Teaching (Doctrine)

THREE THINGS TO AVOID

Psalm 1:1 (Related Admonitions)

I.   The Counsel of the Ungodly
II. The Way of Sinners
III. The Seat of the Scornful

THE PRICE OF A NATION'S HEALING

2 Chronicles 7:14 (Related Conditions)

I.   A Humbling of Self

II. A Return to Prayer

III. A Seeking after God

IV. A Returning to Prayer

THE BELIEVER'S RELATION TO THE TRIUNE GOD

John 4:16 (Related Doctrines)

I. The Son prays for the believers.

II. The Father gives to the believer.

III. The Holy Spirit abides with the believer.

THE SON AND THE FATHER

John 14:6-9 (Related Doctrines)

I. The Son is the way to the Father, v.6.

II. The Son is the revelation of the Father, v.7.

III. The Son is one with the Father, v.9.

THE CONDITIONS FOR ANSWERED PRAYER

John 15:7 (Related Conditions)

I. That we Abide in Christ

II. That Christ's Word Abides in us

APOSTOLIC WORK

Acts 5:42 (Related Ideas)

I. The Regularity of Apostolic Work — Daily

II. The Sphere of Apostolic Work — In the Temple and House

III. The Methods of Apostolic Work — Teaching/Preaching

IV. The Theme of Apostolic Work — Jesus Christ

From an examination of these examples, along with the texts, three things will be noted:

- The divisions are derived from the text.
- The points in the outline are arranged in the same order that they occur in the text.

- The only change made, if any, is in the wording of the divisions, and this is done only when it is needed to make the unity that exits between the parts more evident and easier to remember.

The word "analysis" means "a taking apart," and this is exactly the meaning given to the word in its application to text division. To analyze a text is simply to separate its parts so as to note and examine them separately. In this type, the whole is exactly the sum of the parts. One begins with a whole (a text) and displays its parts. In some texts the parts are obvious as in 1 Timothy 4:12. In other texts the lines of separation are not so clear and must be diligently sought as in Acts 5:42 where such relations as time, place, method and theme must be perceived.

Biographical sermons are effective because... all of us are interested in the successes and even the failures of others.

Sometimes a difficult text will reveal its hidden parts when a series of questions is applied such as: Who is the speaker? Why is this said? Who is addressed? What is required? What are the conditions of success? What lessons are taught? What promises are made? What ideas are expressed? What doctrines are taught? What qualities are displayed? There are many possible questions that can be used in analysis; these are a few for the sake of illustration. The text itself will often suggest its own questions. In most cases, however, the texts suitable for analytic division will be quite easy to treat due to the fact no change is made in the order of the points.

2. Synthesis, or "putting together," involves a rearrangement of points or the construction of an outline from points supplied by a text. With a synthetic method of development, material would be arranged to suit the purpose of the sermon or the pattern of the sermon composition without thought of the order of the points in the text. Here the whole is more than the sum of the parts, as a building is more than a pile of stones because the building, in addition to the material, has a design. In the analytic sermon, the text is the source of material. Analysis is like classifying the strata of marble in a quarry; synthesis is building a structure out of that same marble. Classifying a rubber tree as roots, truck, branches and leaves would be analysis; making an automobile tire would be synthesis.

Care must be taken not to make hasty inferences that do not harmonize with the teaching of Scripture as a whole.

Often the aim of a sermon or the rules of sermon organization make expedient the rearrangement of the material in the text. The last clause of the text may be made the first point and the first clause the last point in the outline in order to have progress and climax in the sermon. Sometimes a minor theme in a text may be made the major theme in the sermon and then some of the material in the text is ignored. The true meaning of the text is not corrupted or compromised, but only that part of the text is utilized that is relevant to the aim of the sermon. Sometimes a design is superimposed upon the material of the text. The biblical material for the outline is from the text, but the total design is invented. Three kinds of synthetic textual sermon outlines have been described: inverted order outlines, minor theme outlines, and superimposed design outlines. Consider these examples:

- **INVERTED ORDER**
  PERFECT MANHOOD IN CHRIST
  Ephesians 4:13
  I.   Perfect manhood is the Christian's aim.
  II. Perfect manhood is seen in Christ.
  III. Perfect manhood is achieved by unity with and knowledge of Christ.

In the text of the above example there are three points: A, B, and C. In the outline they are arranged: B, C, A, because this order is homiletically expedient. The ways of achieving anything should not be treated until what one is to achieve has been proposed. So the first division treats the aim, the second the pattern, and the third the method of achievement, though the order of the points in the text was different.

An expository sermon, like any true sermon, is delivered with persuasion as its principal aim.

- **MINOR THEME**
  RECONCILIATION
  Colossians 1:20-21
  - The Instrument of Reconciliation —
    The Blood of His Cross
  - The Scope of Reconciliation —
    Things in earth or things in heaven
  - The Power of Reconciliation —
    Enmity of mind and wicked works

The real theme of the above text and its context is the "preeminence of Christ," but "reconciliation" is a minor theme that suits the purpose of the present sermon. In the following example, the real theme of the text is "victory over worry," but without doing injustice to the truth or the author's purpose, an outline could treat a minor theme:

* THREE WAYS TO TALK TO GOD
  Philippians 4:6
  I.   Conversation (Prayer)
  II. Supplication (Request)
  III. Adoration (Thanksgiving)

Here a further synthesis is accomplished by the use of parallelism: each word in the outline is a noun and ends with the suffix "tion." If the reader is confused, let him at this point recall that the analytic treatment of the text takes the text as it is with the same order of points, omitting nothing and

Argument alone will not penetrate the fortress of human will.

adding nothing to the design, and in which the main theme of the text is the main theme of the outline.

* SUPERIMPOSED DESIGN
  THE LADDER OF GOD'S ABILITY
  Ephesians 3:20

Introduction: God's working is according to the power that works in us. That working power in us is faith. As faith climbs to each succeeding rung of the ladder of God's power, a fuller view is seen.

I.   God is able to do what we ask.
II. God is able to do what we think.
III. God is able to do all we ask or think.
IV. God is able to do above all we ask or think.
V.   God is able to do abundantly above all we ask or think.
VI. God is able to do exceeding abundantly above all we ask or think.

Here the idea of a ladder is superimposed upon the text to make the sermon more vivid. The meaning of the text is not corrupted or compromised whatever. The truths are the same except that they are given a new framework and rearranged to make an ascending scale. The value of such a treatment should be clearly manifested.

THREE RED-LETTER DAYS ON THE CHRISTIAN CALENDAR
Philippians 1:5-6
I.   The First Day of Conversion
II. The Present Day of Opportunity
III. The Last Day of Christ's Coming

Here the idea of a calendar with red letter days on it is superimposed on the text and here again for the purpose of working the plan more vivid. The secret of good preaching is to make men see as well as hear.

THE CHRISTIAN'S ATTIRE
Colossians 3:12-14
I.   The Turban of Humility —

Humbleness of Mind, Meekness
II. The Tunic of Kindness — Kindness, Compassion
III. The Sandals of Longsuffering — Longsuffering
IV. The Cloak of Forgiveness
V. The Sash of Love

Here greater vividness is achieved by the use of articles of clothing to represent the qualities of Christian character. The superimposed design is suggested by the words of the text, "put on." The articles of attire are arbitrary but the treatment is textual nevertheless and perfectly true to the meaning of the author.

Many texts must, of necessity, be treated synthetically because there is in them no ready order and arrangement of the points. So by analysis, the points of the text are discovered and stated on paper just as they occur to the preacher. Then they are studied until some relationship is seen between them. Finally, the points are studied in order to find some design into which they may be arranged. The synthetic sermon begins with analysis in order to separate all the points, but the analysis is only in the first stage of preparation. Before the sermon is ready for delivery, the points have to be built into a suitable design or arrangement.

The expository sermon that is fully based upon the Scripture has more weight of divine authority and is more likely to be effective.

Chapter Seven

Constructing an Expository Sermon

An expository sermon is a discourse...

...based on a portion of Scripture, occupied mainly with exposition, wholly restricted in the outline to the chosen passage, and delivered with a view of persuasion.

Four features characterize an expository sermon:

1. The text of an expository sermon provides the material for all the divisions and subdivisions. But not only is the division structure provided by the text; the elaboration, or exposition, also is mainly derived from the passage of Scripture chosen for the text.

The whole purpose of preaching is to influence people's lives and decisions by divine truth.

2. The text of an expository sermon is usually longer than the text of a textual or a topical sermon. In fact, the text will usually be a paragraph or a chapter, and sometimes it will be a whole book of the Bible. However, occasionally a single verse is so full and meaningful that it will be sufficient to provide all the material for the sermon.

3. The expository sermon is a treatment of the passage of Scripture. Topical and textual sermons are treatments of the subject. Though the textual sermon gets its main headings from the text, it is really a treatment of a subject as suggested by a text, and the subject is the principal thing. An expository sermon will have a subject, but the subject is subordinate to the text; the text is the principal thing.

4. Finally, in the expository sermon, the Scripture passage is chosen first and the subject derived afterward. In the other sermon types, the subject usually is selected first, and the Scripture text is found afterward. The reason for this is that the expository sermons are most frequently preached in series or courses and consequently the individual sermon is selected because of its relationship to the others in the series, not because it develops a pre-selected subject. Of course, expository sermons may be preached as occasional sermons as well as in a series. But even when this is the case, the Scripture passage is selected because it contains a noteworthy story, parable, conversation, incident, or biographical sketch, or it is one of the chapters that are well known for their appeal or practical application.

Achieving permanent results in preaching depends upon moving the will as much as the emotions.

There are some other things that need to be said about expository sermons for the sake of clarification that many books on homiletics neglect to say. This can best be done here by answering six questions that have frequently been asked in classes and at convention seminars:

1. **Is it necessary for the exposition to follow the order of the verses in the text?** No, it is not necessary to follow the order of the text. This natural order may be followed if it is the logical order already. This would be the method of analysis. But if the text order is not the logical order for discourse, the order may be changed to suit the purpose of the sermon. This would be the method of synthesis. (*Analysis* and *synthesis* were described in the first chapter under "textual sermon construction." Analysis and synthesis may be applied to expository sermon construction, also.)

The Bible should always have first place, and should always be consulted first in prayer and meditation before other sources.

2. **Will the expository sermon always be of the nature of a lecture seeking only to explain and instruct, or do exhortation and application have a place?** A sermon and lecture are two different things. A lecture instructs or entertains; a sermon should instruct and it may entertain, but its main objective is to persuade. An expository lecture is delivered for the purpose of teaching the Word. An expository sermon, like any true sermon, is delivered with persuasion as its principal aim. The expository sermon then has room for dramatization, vivid illustration, and forceful delivery.

3. **Is unity necessary in an expository sermon?** Yes, unity is essential to any sermon of whatever type. A discourse without unity is not really a sermon because unity and climax are necessary for the best success in persuasion. Therefore, for expository sermons, texts should be selected that have unity of thought.

4. Is it necessary to treat all the material in a long text? No, only the material in the text that is related, or that is deemed appropriate to the occasion, needs to be treated. It is better for the sermon if the unrelated portions of the Scripture passage are omitted from the discussion.

5. Is it permissible to quote parallel passages from other parts of the Bible in an expository sermon? Yes, it is permissible to quote parallel passages to support any point in the sermon, provided that the point is based on some statement or inference found in the regular text of the sermon. Obviously, there must not be too many of these quotations or the text will be lost from sight. Furthermore, quotations must not be expounded upon; they are merely to be quoted because the exposition is of the text, not of the parallel passages.

All professionals must devote significant time to their work, and God will provide the needed strength, wisdom, and inspiration.

6. Can illustrations of any type be used in an expository sermon, or must they, too, be derived from the text? Any illustrations whatever may be used, but if they can be drawn from the text, context, historical background, or preacher's experience, the sermon will be more compact and instructive. Success is more important than compactness, so the preacher's taste should be the guide.

The remainder of this chapter will be devoted to explaining the several ways of constructing the expository sermon outline, the ways of building the elaboration or exposition, and the method of preparing the whole sermon step-by-step.

Varieties of Expository Sermons

There are six varieties of expository sermons: (1) doctrinal, (2) ethical, (3) inferential, (4) biographical, (5) analogical, (6) propositional. The terms, "topical" "textual" and "expository" describe the methods of constructing a sermon as related to the text; these latter terms describe the kinds of subject matter with which the text deals. A sermon is "expository" because it expounds and is limited to a consecutive passage of Scripture, but its subject may be doctrinal, ethical, biographical, and so on. These terms will be defined and explained, and the definitions will be used consistently throughout this book to refer to the same things. When the terms are used by other writers, they may mean something different, but as long as terms are used consistently by the same author, there is no confusion.

Experience is of value to the person who has the experience, but not of much value to others— unless it is shared by so many as to be common human phenomenon.

1. The *doctrinal* expository sermon is designed to expound the doctrinal teaching of a text, and the unity of the sermon is based upon related doctrines or related aspects of a single doctrine as the text permits. In this book the term "doctrinal" will be used only to describe sermons that point out, explain, and apply doctrines. The term will not apply to sermons that primarily aim to prove a position. Such proof sermons will be called "propositional" even when the subject matter is doctrinal. The following will

illustrate the nature of a doctrinal expository sermon:

JUSTIFICATION
Romans 5:1-9
I.   The Need for Justification
     A. Man's lack of strength, v.6
     B. Man's sinful state, v.8
II. The Provision for Justification
     A. God's love, v. 8
     B. Christ's death, v.6
III. The Appropriation of Justification—by Faith, v.1
IV. The Results of Justification
     A. Access to grace, v.2
     B. Peace with God, v.1
     C. Salvation from wrath, v.9
     D. Victory in tribulation, v.3
     E. Development of character, v.3-5
         1. Patience to experience
         2. Experience to hope
         3. Hope to shamelessness

The above example is **expository** because it is taken entirely from one passage of Scripture. It is **synthetic** in its construction because the points are not arranged in the same order in which they occur in the text. And it is **doctrinal** because its aim is to explain and enforce the doctrine of justification. Doctrinal preaching is important to help people avoid the temptation to become involved in false cults or to dabble in religions fads.

2. The *ethical* **expository sermon is designed to discover, explain, and enforce rules of right Christian conduct.** In the latter chapters of Paul's epistles and in some parts of the Gospels, the material pertains to the conduct of the believer's life. Sermons built upon texts

dealing with the Christian's morals and behavior are called ethical sermons. The divisions of ethical sermons consist of related rules of behavior or related aspects of one ethical idea. Note the following examples:

PERSONAL HABITS
Romans 14:12-21
I. Personal habits are accountable to God, v.12.
II. Personal habits are not to be judged by men, v.13.
III. Personal habits must not offend the weak, vv.15, 20, 21.
IV. Personal habits are subordinate to Kingdom interests, vv.17, 19.

A CHRISTIAN'S RESPONSIBILITY AS A CITIZEN
Romans 13:1-10
I. Regarding Civil Obedience, vv.1-5
   A. Implicit obedience, v.2
   B. Fearless obedience, vv.3, 4
II. Regarding Financial Obligation, vv.6-8
   A. To the state, vv.6, 7
   B. To every creditor, v.8
III. Regarding Social Morals, vv.9, 10
   A. In accordance with Bible ethics, v.9
   B. In accordance with love's law, v.10

There is a tendency for some preachers to neglect ethical preaching, but a large place is given in the New Testament to the regulation of Christian conduct. To neglect ethical preaching is to overlook much of the Holy Word. If the neglect is due to a fear that ethical sermons will be poorly received, that fear is unfounded. Ethics in a *topical* sermon might be made offensive because it might be thought to be personal, but in an expository sermon, suspicion of personal antagonism is very unlikely. In addition, the expository sermon that is fully based upon the Scripture has more weight of divine authority and is more likely to be effective.

3. The inferential, or "observational," expository sermon is designed so that the divisions are derived from inferences drawn from the facts and the details of a narrative text. A narrative text is one that tells a story, such as history or parable. In a story text, ideas or facts are not directly stated, but must be inferred from the conduct of the characters in the narrative, their conversations, and their success or failure. The inferences may be of a doctrinal or ethical nature, but the sermon is called inferential if the points are derived by inference from a narrative text instead of by direct statement by the author of the Bible book. Inferences, when they are carefully made, are almost as binding as direct statements and they are often more vivid to the hearers. Note the following example:

The Bible, when it is correctly interpreted, is the final authority for true Christians.

A YOUNG MAN'S RUIN
2 Kings 5:20-27
I.   Sin begins with covetousness, v.26.
II. Sin leads to other sins, v.25.
III. Sin cannot be kept secret, v.26.
IV. Sin's allurement is deceptive, vv. 20, 27.
V.   Sin received sure punishment, v.27.

Notice that none of these facts about sin are directly stated by the author of Second Kings, but they are inferred from the details of the story and from the conversations between the characters in the story. Nearly all expository preaching from texts in historical sections of the Bible will be treated by related inferences. Paul says about Israel's history, "Now all these things happened unto them for examples" (1 Corinthians 10:11). Therefore, we are given liberty to construct inferential sermons. Care must be taken, however, not to make hasty inferences that do not harmonize with the teaching of Scripture as a whole. Wild spiritualizing must also be avoided.

Preachers must go to the pulpit prayerfully, determined to turn sinners to righteousness and believers to higher planes of faith and service.

4. **The biographical expository sermon is one in which the successes and/or failures, or the good and/or bad characteristics of a Bible character are discovered, discussed, and presented for the hearer to imitate or avoid.** Again, the facts deduced may be doctrinal or ethical in nature, but if the facts are drawn from an appraisal of biography instead of being directly stated, the sermon will be called "biographical." Observe the following example from the biographical sketch of Cornelius in Acts 10.

WHY GOD USED CORNELIUS
Acts 10:1-8
I. He was a man of character, vv. 1-2.
    A. He was a strong man, moral though a soldier.
    B. He was a devout man.
    C. He was a generous man.
    D. He was an influential man, "with all his house."

II. He was a man of prayer, vv. 2, 3, 4.
   A. He prayed always.
   B. He prayed with faith.
   C. He prayed with yieldedness.
III. He was a man of action who immediately obeyed God, vv. 5-8.

Biographical sermons are quite effective because of the human interest aspect; all of us are interested in the successes and even the failures of others. Biographical sermons are splendid for preaching to young people, for they can be made very vivid and dramatic. Care must be taken, however, to ensure that a biographical sermon is not simply an array of facts about an ancient person; it must have application to real, present-day problems and conditions.

An introduction is striking when it goes straight to a point of interest for the hearers and when the idea is expressed in an original manner.

5. The analogical expository sermon is designed so that the divisions are related parts of an analogy. An analogy is a comparison of things that may not appear similar, yet possess similar traits or characteristics. Life is said to be analogous to a sea voyage, not because there is outward similarity between them, but because they have similar characteristics such as a start, peaceful and turbulent experiences, a purpose, and an end. Note the following illustration:

THE CHRISTIAN'S RACE OF LIFE
Hebrews 12:1,2

I. The Spectators at the Race:
   The martyrs of chapter 11 who have run before us
II. The Training for the Race:
   Putting off the heavy garments of sin
III. The Gait of the Race:
   Patient striving
VI. The Judge of the Race:
   Jesus, the Starter and Finisher
V. The Reward for the Race:
   Sharing with Christ His exaltation

The actual activities of a Christian life do not outwardly resemble the running of a race, but there are characteristics of each that resemble, such as spectators, training, patient striving, a judge and a reward. This type of sermon can be made very vivid and is usually easy to remember. The Bible contains many such analogies, nearly all of which make excellent sermon texts. Analogical sermons are very good for children and young people.

In almost every case, the sermon that is too long is too long in the introduction.

6. **The propositional expository sermon is designed so that the divisions are the arguments in the proof of a proposition.** The New Testament writers who wrote to instruct and encourage members of infant churches in the midst of a hostile world devote a considerable portion of their epistles and Gospels to arguments against false teaching. Many of those same controversies are still raging today, and many of the arguments are as valid today as they were when they

first were written. Achieving permanent results in preaching depends upon moving the will as much as the emotions. Therefore, there is a large place for argument in the preaching of this day of science and reason. Argument alone will not penetrate the fortress of human will, but argument is a large part of the human element in successful preaching. For some purposes and to some audiences, the preacher can well make the whole sermon a proof of a clearly stated proposition. A sermon is not propositional because it has a proposition (theme) or because it contains argument, but it is propositional when *all the divisions* are parts of the proof of a single proposition. Consider the following example:

THE RESURRECTION OF CHRIST

1 Corinthians 15:3-23

Proposition: That Jesus Christ arose from the dead

I. There are many witnesses to the fact.
    A. Peter saw Him.
    B. The Twelve saw Him.
    C. Five hundred brethren at once saw Him.
    D. Paul, by revelation, saw Him.
II. The opposite conclusion is absurd.
    A. Preaching would be vain.
    B. Faith would be vain.
    C. Holy men would be false witnesses.
    D. Faithful believers would be deluded sinners.
    E. All the righteous dead perished.
III. Christ's Resurrection is a theological necessity: There must be a second Adam to nullify the sin and death imputed through the transgression of the first Adam.

Methods of Elaboration

A sermon without a skeleton is like a man without a back-bone or like a building without a framework. But just as a man must be more than bones and a building more than rafters, so must a sermon be more than skeleton. The sermon skeleton must be clothed with living flesh. There must be an elaboration of the skeletal ideas that constitute the sermon divisions. Many homiletical writers recognize six methods of elaboration. Although there may be other methods, the following six will be discussed:

1. One form is *verbal* elaboration which consists of defining the words of the text that are not completely clear or of explaining the idioms and syntax of the grammar. There are two reasons for the need of this kind of elaboration. The English Bible is a translation from other languages, and, while it is quite reliable for all matters of doctrine, its teachings are much clearer when read in the original languages. For instance, Philippians 1:27 is made clearer and more interesting by explaining the word "conversation" means "citizenship." It is then seen that the following verses contain instructions regarding good Christian citizenship that applied quite appropriately to the people of Philippi who lived in a Roman colony and who had more than average interest in citizenship. Verbal elaboration need not always be concerned with the original languages, but may be con-

Preachers who have had insufficient time to prepare should simply ask God's help and go ahead and preach; an apology does not make a hastily prepared sermon any better.

cerned also with the meanings and grammar of English words.

2. Another form of elaboration, called *contextual*, **consists of using portions of the context to throw light on the text.** Usually the explanations will come from the immediate context, but occasionally a verse from another part of the same book will be valuable for solving a doubtful meaning. In Hebrews 12:1 the phrase "cloud of witnesses" may be misleading if it is not interpreted in the light of the preceding eleventh chapter. The "witnesses" may be thought to refer to any onlookers who observe critically the manner of the Christian life, but the context shows that the "witnesses" are the heroes of faith of the eleventh chapter. This reference to the context is not made alone as a matter of interpretation, but as a matter of elaboration, connecting Scripture passages in a way that is not obvious on the surface.

If the first rule for the conclusion is "Be clear," then the second is "Be specific."

3. A further form of elaboration, called *historical*, **con**sists of relating historical events or conditions pertaining either to the people addressed or to the author. An elaboration of the second chapter of Colossians should include an explanation of the Gnostic heresy with which certain teachers were confusing the Christians of Colosse. Philippians 1:20-25 may be partly elaborated by explaining some details of Paul's imprisonment at Rome and his impending martyrdom. Such historical and biographical data can be learned from good commentaries or Bible dictionaries.

4. Yet another form of elaboration consists of the quotation of *parallel passages.* Scripture is very frequently explained by Scripture. A meager statement may be strengthened or made more lucid by the quotation of a more detailed statement ,of the same fact from another part of Scripture. A passage of doubtful meaning can often be made clear by a parallel passage that is not ambiguous. Here a word of caution is needful. Parallel passages in an expository sermon must not be more than quotations, for the exposition is of the text, not the parallel passages. One quotation can easily lead to another until the discussion is far removed from the original text.

5. The text may be elaborated by the use of *illustrations.* These illustrations may come from the Bible, history, experience, or modern life. By all means, let there be illustrations in the expository sermon because they make the sermon both clear and interesting. Illustrations help to avoid dryness that might characterize an expository sermon that is too largely explanation. The success of Beecher, Spurgeon, and Moody was in no small degree due to an ability to use pertinent illustrations. Preachers should study good books on the art of illustrating sermons. The most important thing in illustrating the expository sermon is that the illustrations be appropriate; in other words, they should actually illuminate some point in the text.

There is no reason to say that a point or story is the last unless the speaker wishes to assure the hearers that the tribulation is nearly over.

6. Finally, and considerably important, *application* is a form of elaboration. It has been observed that application is actually where the sermon begins. The whole purpose of preaching is to influence people's lives and decisions by divine truth. Producing Christian conversion, godly living, and brotherly love is far more important than making admirers. Let us "implore men to be reconciled to God," that we may be the worthy successors of those who did not cease to "warn everyone night and day with tears."

For a sermon to be of highest quality, it should be clear, precise, beautiful, forceful, and interesting.

Expository preaching, however, is not solely teaching or didactic. The expository sermon need not be delivered in the calm tone of the classroom; it can be and should be, at least in places, forceful and impassioned. By all means, let the expository sermon be adapted to modern needs and problems and not simply a discussion of ancient people and conditions. There are two ways of making applications. They may be made along with each point in the sermon, or they may be made all together at the end of the sermon. It seems better in most cases to make the applications after each point as the sermon progresses and then to summarize the principal applications at the end.

Organizing Expository Sermons

One of the most effective methods for organizing the textual materials in the preparation of expository sermons is using the *key word*. For instance, every substantial text will deal with a certain number of related ideas. Usually a certain word will tie these ideas together. One text might set forth a number of rules; another lessons, steps, blessings, warnings, evidences, and so forth.

In Acts 8, a sermon on Philip and the eunuch might have the title, "Characteristics of Successful Witnessing." The *key word* would be "characteristics." All key words are plural. There will be one of such for each main division of the sermon. For instance, you might preach on the subject "Four Steps to Salvation." Each of the main divisions will be a *step* toward the realization of salvation. In Philippians 3, Paul deals with Christian maturity, giving his own testimony (11-15). A sermon on this text might be, "Marks of Christian Maturity." "*Marks*" is the key word. At least four of these marks can be found:

An hour of meditation is more fruitful than two hours of reading commentaries.

MARKS OF CHRISTIAN MATURITY
Philippians 3:12-15
Introduction: The following attitudes **mark** or
 indicate Christian maturity.
I.   Humble Self Appraisal, v. 12
     A. Not perfect
     B. Not yet attained
II. Forgetting the Past, v. 13
     A. What we do not forget
     B. What we must forget
III. Keying on the Present, v. 14
     A. Singleness of purpose
     B. Perseverance in a cause
IV. Focusing on the Future, v. 14
     A. A matchless goal
     B. An eternal prize

CHARACTERISTICS OF SUCCESSFUL WITNESSING

Acts 8:26-38

Introduction: Philip demonstrates the characteristics of successful witnessing for Christ.

I. Sensitivity to Divine Guidance, vv. 26, 29
II. Beginning with the Subject's Interest, v. 30, 35
III. Presenting Christ from the Scriptures, vv. 31-35
VI. Pressing for true Saving Faith, vv. 37, 38

A sermon on the Christian's growth might use the key word, *steps* or *gains*. A text warning believers might include such key words as *warnings, dangers, admonitions, pitfalls*. A sermon on God's abundance could employ such key words as *promises, blessings, provisions, benefits, advantages*, or even *rewards*. The latter key word, *rewards*, could be used in a sermon on the Parable of the Talents using the title, "Rewards and Faithfulness." A text from Timothy might set forth certain *lessons*. From Acts, the sermon might reveal *facts*. A Bible character sermon might well display *habits*, and so forth.

Sermons were made for people, not people for sermons.

Steps in Expository Sermon Preparation

Books on homiletics that give all the needed facts, classifications, and general information regarding scientific preaching too often fail to demonstrate the actual steps in sermon preparation. This is especially true regarding the preparation of expository sermons. The following steps of preparation appear in their natural order, but they may easily be changed to suit a preacher's personal preference.

1. Select an appropriate passage of Scripture for a text. The selection may be made because it is the next portion of Scripture in a series, because it is the leading of the Holy Spirit, or because it is the obvious text to meet a known need of the people.

2. Read the text through carefully several times in the New King James Version or other reliable translation; then read it in the original language or in several modern translations.

3. Write down your thoughts, regardless of order or relevance. This will include explanations, proofs, and illustrations.

4. Consult a good exegetical commentary. This should not be done, however, until you have exhausted your ability to find original thoughts.

5. Examine the material until one theme stands out above the rest or until one common theme is detected. This may be done by listing all the possible themes and then trying each until all but one are eliminated. It will help to examine the material in the following manner. Are there related doctrines? ...related ethical instructions? ...related inferences or observations? ...related biographical traits? ...related arguments in the proof of a proposition?

People are little interested in academic or abstract theological matters; they are interested in finding help for their needs, problems, and daily lives.

6. Eliminate all the material that does not relate to the theme in some practical way.

7. **Arrange the remaining material in an outline of main divisions and subdivisions so that they have coherence, progress, and climax.** The main divisions are the big related ideas; the subdivisions are the lesser ideas that are related closely to one of the main divisions.

8. **Prepare an introduction and a conclusion for the sermon.**

9. **Create a title for the sermon, which may or may not be the same as the theme.** The title may be shorter than the theme, but it should accurately convey the nature of the sermon theme. The title should get the attention of the hearers.

10. **Finally, study the outline until the sermon can be delivered without the use of notes.**

All of this seems to be, and actually is, time consuming. However, all professionals must devote significant time to their work, and God will provide the needed strength, wisdom, and inspiration.

Chapter Eight

Gathering Your Materials

Sermon materials are most frequently classified as four types...

...*explanation, argument, illustration, and application.* Clarifications of these types follow:

1. All sermons should contain some *explanation*. This is true of all three types of sermons: topical, textual, and expository. A proposition can be more successfully enforced if the hearers have first been shown what the proposition means and that it is reasonable and scriptural. People who accept propositions without explanation will be easy prey for false teachers. Some sermons require more explanation than others, and some types of sermons will be naturally more explanatory than other types. For instance, an expository sermon will usually contain more explanation than a topical sermon. Teaching is not possible without explanation. There has been no lack of exhortation from the pulpit, so many are becoming very eager to be

The greatest value of expression is its power to clothe words with life and fullness of meaning so that people may be moved to action.

taught in the Scripture. The principal source of explanation is the Bible itself. Another source of explanation is Christian literature, such as commentaries, concordances, Bible dictionaries, and books on Bible subjects.

Preachers must believe that God is going to honor His Word and accomplish the purpose of the sermon.

Preachers who expect to be heard by others ought to be willing to respect the sermons and writings of other Christian preachers and teachers. But the Bible should always have first place, and should always be consulted first in prayer and meditation before other sources are consulted.

2. A second kind of material is argument. Argument is a process by which it is proved, demonstrated, or inferred that a certain proposition is true or false. The New Testament epistles are filled with argument that show some propositions to be true and some false. From this it can at least be strongly inferred that argument has a place in Christian preaching. Preaching ought to appeal to human will as well as to the intellect or to the emotions. The Lord said by the mouth of Isaiah, "Come, let us *reason* together..." (Isaiah 1:18). Paul the apostle *reasoned* with Felix as he shared the gospel. Following are some of the most practical forms of argument:

- **Deduction.** This is reasoning from the general to the specific, that is, from a law or an authoritative premise to a specific case. It is accepted that the statement, "Whatsoever a man soweth, that shall he also reap," is authoritative because it is revealed in the Holy Scriptures that were divinely inspired.

John Doe is known to be sowing evil and violence, so it is reasoned from the accepted premise that John Doe will reap evil and violence. This reasoning can be used only where all persons accept the major premise as true.

- **Induction.** This is reasoning from the specific to the general, the converse of deduction. If an opponent does not accept the Bible statement about sowing and reaping, wide evidence must be gathered to show that the axiom is true because it is known to be true in a sufficient number of specific cases. If every person who is known to have sown violence has reaped the same, then a general rule or law is established. This reasoning is inductive. Care must be taken to ensure that a law will not be formulated on insufficient evidence and experimentation.

The subjects treated in many churches are so unrelated and disconnected that people have no chance to obtain an organized picture of any doctrine or book.

- **Cause to effect** (*a priori*). In this manner, we reason that God, who is a loving, all-powerful and all-wise cause, will effect the working together for good in the lives of His people who are yielded to Him. In this reasoning, the cause must be known and admitted by all concerned. For the Christian who has faith, God is accepted as the only infinite cause whose attributes are those revealed in the Bible. This argument has little value in argument with non-Christians.

- **Effect to cause** (*a posteriori*). When we reason from

design in nature and providence that there must be an all-powerful and an all-wise God, we are reasoning from effect to cause. If we reason that because there have been conversions in a Christian service, God's Spirit has been present to convict, it is "*a posteriori*" argument. If we reason that, because God's Spirit is present, there will be conviction of sin, this is a "*priori*" argument.

- **From the lesser to the greater (*a fortiori*).** By this we mean that something that is valid in an unlikely situation will be much more valid in a likely situation. In Matthew 6:30 Jesus argued "a fortiori" when He said, "Wherefore, if God so clothed the grass of the field, which today is and tomorrow is cast into the oven: shall he not much more clothe you, O ye of little faith?" By this method we may reason that, if the heathen make great personal sacrifices for heathen deities, how much more should Christians who serve the true God give themselves wholly to His service.

> *If we ask God for results, seek results, and believe in results, all Satan's hosts cannot stop the advance of the gospel.*

- **Analogy.** This is arguing that what is true in one realm is probably true in another realm. Because the lily bulb that is put in the ground is able after dying to come forth to new life, it is reasoned by analogy that man, likewise, in a higher realm will probably come forth from the grave with new life. This is never a conclusive form of proof, but it can be used to strengthen a proposition that has other forms of argument in its favor. For almost every spiritual law or fact, there is an analogy in the physical realm.

- **Tradition.** This is arguing that there is a presumption in favor of an established institution, tradition, or practice. This does not mean that all old and traditional things are true, but that they are to be respected until something demonstrably superior can be found to take the place of the old and traditional. We reason from tradition that the doctrines of the orthodox historic church are to be accepted as valid. We maintain this position until it can be shown from the Bible to the satisfaction of the majority of spiritual and thinking Christians that these doctrines are false, and that there are more satisfactory doctrines to replace the old.

- **Testimony.** This is one of the most common kinds of argument. It is used in all courts of law and is a strong form of proof under controlled conditions. For testimony to be valid, the witness must be examined as to character, competence, and familiarity with the facts. A witness of deceitful character is of no value. A witness must also be competent to judge concerning the facts, in other words, intelligent; it is even better if the witness is an expert in the matter on which testimony is given. Furthermore, the witness must have first-hand testimony; it must not be hearsay. Finally, there must be a sufficient number of witnesses to ensure that there is no delusion or mistake due to the unreliability of the senses.

The incidents and discourses of the life of Christ provide opportunity for discussing most all of the needs and problems of the Christian life and service.

- **Experience.** This argument is used by many, but it does not have great value because almost anything can be proved by somebody's experience. Experience is of value to the person who has the experience, but not of much value to others unless the experience is shared by so many as to be common human phenomenon. Then it is referred to as the argument from *consensus.*

- **Authority.** Argument from authority is also a common form and has weight when the authorities are accepted as such by all parties. The Bible, when it is correctly interpreted, is the final authority for true Christians.

- **Reductio ad absurdum.** This is reducing the opponent's proposition to the absurd. When the Pharisees insisted that Jesus was a sinner because He healed on the Sabbath, He reduced their premise to the absurd by showing them that they helped their animals that fell into a ditch on the Sabbath, but were not willing to help human sufferers on the Sabbath.

- **Process of elimination.** This consists of listing all possible alternatives and disposing of them one by one until only one is left. Consider the three possible statements about God relative to love: God loves no men; God loves only some men; God loves all men. The first is eliminated by the Scripture, "God is love." The second is eliminated by the Scripture, "God is no respecter of persons." So the last only is possible in the light of the Scriptures. There are other forms or argument used in logic, but these are deemed sufficient for this treatise. If a full treatment is desired, let the reader consult a textbook on logic.

3. The third kind of material is *illustration*. Someone has said, "Illustrations are the windows of the sermons." The analogy is a good one, for illustrations do let needed light into the sermon. It is not enough that people hear sermons; they must see them also if the sermon is to stick. Illustrations make it possible for abstract truth to become vivid. Jesus constantly spoke in parables and used such words as salt, light, bread, sheep, vine, king, house, water and mountain to give imagery to His spiritual ideas. A preacher who neglects to illustrate will invariably be dry and hard to understand. There should be one illustration for every abstract idea in a sermon.

> *A series, like an individual sermon, should be selected to coincide with the needs or interests of the people.*

There are several kinds of illustrations, all of which should be used with variety in the sermon:

- The **one word** illustration. To say that the Bible is "bread" is such an illustration; or that a Christian is "salt"; or that the gospel is "light"; or that God is a "judge." There are hundreds of words that make apt illustrations.

- **Analogy.** In addition to being a form of proof, analogy is an excellent kind of illustration. Likening the various duties of a farmer to the work of the ministry, or the growth of a plant to a Christian's growth, or an ocean voyage to the course of human life, would be using analogy in illustration.

- **Anecdote.** This is the use of a true incident in a person's own experience or the reported experience of another. Anecdote is the most common kind of illustration used by many preachers, but it should not be overused; when too many are told, there may be insufficient time for other necessary materials. Many of the points will be better illustrated by word pictures or brief analogies.

- **The story.** This differs from an anecdote in that a story is not an actual incident, but fiction, or at least not sufficiently verified to be told as truth. Stories should not be told as anecdotes and certainly not as real experiences of the preacher. A preacher may invent stories or take them from fiction. Stories should not be told merely to entertain, but to illustrate in an apt manner doctrines or applications in the sermon. The story often differs very little from a parable.

Preaching is not mere communication; it always has a goal to motivate hearers to make a decision and to take some form of action.

There are many sources of illustrations, including the following:

- **The Bible.** This is one of the best sources of illustration because it is most adaptable to the sermon, being of like nature with the other materials.
- **Science.** Many scientific laws and facts may be used as sermon illustrations. The opposite magnetic poles may be used to illustrate the conflict between the flesh and the Spirit.
- **Nature.** All of nature declares the glory of God; observant preachers can make good use of this resource.
- **Fiction.** The great works of classic literature are filled with stories that can be used in sermons.

- **Poetry.** A well-chosen poem can enhance the interest and appeal of a sermon.
- **History.** The historic deeds of men and fates of nations make some of the most common illustrations found in the sermons of the world's most successful preachers.
- **Current events.** Of great interest are the latest happenings from the pages of the newspaper and from newscasts. When current events are used, they must be appropriate and relevant.

4. The fourth kind of material is *application* **or persuasion.** It is this material that distinguishes a sermon from a talk or lecture. A sermon should instruct and inspire, but whatever else it does, it should persuade. The preacher seeks action. He deals in life and death decisions and consequences. Preachers must go to the pulpit prayerfully, determined to turn sinners to righteousness and believers to higher planes of faith and service. Then will they truly be ambassadors of God.

If we can make the Scriptures clear, understandable, and memorable, our preaching will accomplish more nearly its divinely intended purpose of changing lives.

The ideal sermon will contain some of each of the four kinds of material. If the sermon is all explanation, it will be too dry. If it is all argument, it will be too contentious. If it is all illustration, it will be too shallow. If it is all application, it will lack substance. If the sermon has a balance of all four materials, it will instruct the mind, impress the will, hold the attention, stir the emotions and move to action, provided it is delivered under the anointing of the Spirit.

Chapter Nine

Preparing an Introduction and Conclusion

We have a tendency to underestimate the value of small things...

...and the introduction and conclusion of a sermon are small parts. However, they are vital to the success of a sermon. Because they are small parts, many preachers overlook their importance. Preachers who quite carefully prepare the body of the sermon leave the introduction and conclusion for the inspiration of the moment of speaking. And while the conclusion may borrow inspiration from the climax, it will, without forethought, lack other desirable qualities.

When we show that the Bible message is timeless and that it speaks powerfully to current situations, we preach it persuasively.

Some writers on homiletics insist that the introduction and conclusion should be given more preparation than any other part of the sermon. This may be going too far in the other direction, but not much. When the desirable qualities of the introduction and conclusion are considered, it will be quite clear why these parts of the sermon need careful preparation.

The Qualities of a Good Introduction

1. First of all, a sermon introduction should be *striking.* Initial impressions are usually lasting and not easy to change. If a sermon is uninteresting in its first few sentences, a preacher will find it difficult to arouse interest later. An introduction is striking when it goes straight to a point of interest for the hearers and when the idea is expressed in an original manner. When the first sentences of a sermon strike the hearers' interest, the preacher gains an attentive audience. If the sermon begins in a dull manner, people may conclude that it is "just another sermon." Preachers will have a much friendlier reception if they let it be known that they have something of value for the people and are not just seeking an audience to hear them speak. It has been said that the introduction should *"start a fire."*

2. An introduction should be *clear.* Hearers may not at first be sufficiently alert to capture abstract or involved concepts. Further, thoughts must be apparent in order that interest may be aroused in the theme. It is hardly possible for people to be interested in a proposition they do not understand. An obscure introduction will give the impression that the whole sermon is to be obscure or over the heads of the people. If sermon content is really quite deep, it needs a clear introduction even more; difficult concepts can be made clear if they are built on a lucid foundation and approached sys-

The Bible, being God's inspired Word for all ages of time, is as relevant today as it was when first penned.

tematically. It makes for clarity in the introduction to give the introduction careful study and meditation.

3. An introduction should have *unity*. The prelude to the sermon should have only one idea because a multiplicity of ideas is inconsistent with both clarity and interest. Having several ideas in the introduction is like having a speaker introduced by several people. Either the first does not make a proper introduction, or the others are an unnecessary waste of time.

> *No one is ever persuaded toward an undefined goal.*

4. An introduction should be *brief*. Everyone resents the person who takes thirty minutes to introduce a speaker. They are also annoyed when that speaker takes half his time approaching the subject. In almost every case, the sermon that is too long is too long in the introduction. In these days of rush and competition, hearers appreciate preachers going straight to the point with as little delay as possible.

5. An introduction should be *modest*. In other words, it should be delivered in a conversational tone of voice and should not be too pretentious or eloquent. When an introduction is too impassioned in tone, the sermon may seem dull by comparison. Or if the intensity and volume are maintained uniformly throughout, it can lead to monotony. When the introduction is too eloquent, the sermon will seem commonplace; if the sermon is equally eloquent, it becomes too saccharine. An introduction can be striking without thunderous volume, excessive eloquence, or pretentious language.

6. **An introduction should be** *unapologetic.* Though the introduction should be modest, it should not include any kind of apology. Anything for which the preacher needs to apologize should be avoided or omitted. Unavoidable states of health and voice or accidents are only accentuated by an apology. Preachers who have had insufficient time to prepare should simply ask God's help and go ahead and preach; an apology does not make a hastily prepared sermon any better. Preachers have delivered effective sermons by God's help in spite of physical weakness or lack of preparation, when the lack of preparation was not due to laziness.

The sermon is not an appendage to worship; it is a part of it.

7. **Finally, a sermon introduction should be** *specific.* An introduction should be prepared for one specific sermon. An introduction that is so general that it can introduce any sermon is not really suitable to introduce any sermon adequately. A good introduction will contain a clear statement of the theme and purpose of the sermon. Obviously, then, a proper introduction must be specifically prepared. While the introduction is related to the sermon, it should not be a part of the body, nor should it predict the material of any of the divisions. An introduction is simply an approach to the theme that prepares the listeners for the sermon and arouses interest.

Finding a Proper Introduction

The following is a series of questions that the preacher asks about his sermon in order to hit upon an introduction. The answer to one of these questions should suggest the introduction that fits the sermon in question.

1. What has the text to do with the context? It is often best to introduce a sermon by showing the context of the scriptural text, especially with a narrative text that may not be clear without some historical background. The story of Naaman the leper is clearer when we know something about the preceding events and the state of affairs between Israel and Syria. Most of the texts in the book of Revelation are meaningless until the surrounding verses or chapters are summarized. This might be true of any text from any part of the Bible.

2. What relation has this sermon to a preceding sermon in a series? Sermons in a course or series can often be best introduced by a brief synopsis or summary of the preceding sermon of the week before.

3. What has this sermon to do with the special day or occasion? If the sermon has been prepared for a special day or event, it will often be introduced best by an explanation of the sentiment or tradition of the occasion.

4. What has this sermon to do with some special need of the congregation? The introduction often will consist of a statement of the need or needs of the congregation, particularly when the sermon has been prepared to meet this need or condition. This is especially effective when the need is generally recognized by the people who are eager to have the need supplied. If the need is not recognized or admitted, it is best to use a different introduction. The preacher may approach the sermon by pointing to the condition and then proposing a sermon that will show the way to a higher spiritual plane, always leading people toward hope.

5. What personal experience has suggested this sermon? If the sermon has been suggested by a personal experience, the preacher may introduce the sermon by briefly telling of the experience and how it suggested the sermon. Such experiences should be told modestly and without superfluous details. This type of introduction should not be used too frequently.

There is no doubt that a preacher's character and quality of life can strongly reinforce his reasoning about righteousness.

6. Why is this sermon of special importance? When a sermon addresses a truly important subject, an introduction may simply call attention to that subject's importance to the hearers. People become interested at once when they see the importance of a subject, but they will not be impressed by such introductions if the sermons prove to be disappointing. This type of introduction can be effective, but it should be used only when the sermon is of special importance. There certainly are a great many highly significant themes in the Holy Scriptures which, if properly treated, are worthy of the time and attention of the hearers.

7. What story or anecdote will introduce this sermon? A truly apt story makes a most attractive introduction. Care must be taken to ensure that the story clearly suggests the sermon theme, and distracting details must be omitted. It is important that the story or anecdote be fresh, for trite anecdotes arouse no interest.

8. What current event will introduce this sermon? Current events are usually quite striking, and they make excellent introductions to sermons when they are relevant to the theme. There is one caution: It is best not to refer to news events that agitate people or that cause mental distress, because people will think about the news and will not follow the sermon.

A preacher may approach a sermon simply by appealing for the attention of the people when there is only a limited time for the sermon. Usually, however, a sermon should have a proper introduction; most people have an aversion to abruptness and are not ready to concentrate on an idea without preparation. In rare cases, an introduction may be omitted when all the time is needed for the sermon.

The Qualities of a Good Conclusion

1. The sermon conclusion should have *clarity.* The conclusion is the part of the sermon that calls for action or decision. It is the most vital part of the sermon, so there must not be any obscurity of thought. A lawyer would never win a case if his appeal to the jury were ambiguous or equivocal. Even a deep sermon must be crystal clear in the conclusion, or it can have no practical success. The great soul winners, without exception, concluded their sermons by making perfectly clear the actions and decisions they were asking hearers to make.

2. The conclusion should have *unity.* If we call on our hearers to do too many things, they are not likely to do any of them. But if we put before them clearly and earnestly just one exhortation, there is good chance of success. The reason some sermons lack unity as well as clarity in the conclusion is that the preacher has no clear expectations of what the sermon should accomplish. Paul reveals to us one of the elements of his success in the words, "This ONE THING I do." If the first rule for the conclusion is "Be clear," then the second is "Be specific."

3. The conclusion should be *brief*. If the sermon has been properly constructed and God is dealing with the hearers, the conclusion need not be long. If the sermon has been weak, a long conclusion will be futile. There is no ironclad rule for the length of the conclusion because "circumstances alter cases," but, if there is any doubt, the preacher should opt for brevity.

The sermon is the preacher's task; the anointing is God's work, and no sermon can ever bring permanent spiritual results without God's anointing.

4. Finally, the sermon conclusion should be *intense*. Intensity does not necessarily mean volume. More important are moral and spiritual intensity, that is, sincere earnestness or godly zeal. A preacher who cannot be intense in his appeal for decisions that have eternal consequences is not "fit for the Kingdom of God."

Types of Conclusions

1. First, there is the *lesson*. This type of conclusion consists of stating the lesson that the sermon teaches. In most sermons, the applications are made within the body of the sermon. But sometimes in doctrinal or propositional sermons, the doctrines are explained or the proposition is proved in the body, and the practical lesson is saved for the conclusion. This will most often be true with teaching sermons that call for no immediate decision at the close, but suggest a final lesson. For instance, in a sermon on the deity of Christ, the body of the sermon may be entirely devoted to proof. However, the preacher may conclude by pointing to the fact that a truly divine Christ is sufficiently able to keep all His promises and sustain His people at all times. By that means a lesson in confidence is taught by what would otherwise be merely a lecture. Avoid concluding a sermon with numerous lessons, for this violates unity and is not effective.

Anointing is a spiritual force of conviction that God puts into a preacher's message that causes it to bring results.

2. Next, there is the *summary.* Also called "recapitulation," a summary is also an effective conclusion for a sermon where no immediate decision is sought, no altar call given. A summary consists of briefly repeating the salient points of a sermon in order to aid retention. If possible, to avoid monotony, the applications should be stated in different words. By all means, the summary should be brief. A summary makes a splendid conclusion for a teaching sermon because repetition greatly aids the learning process.

3. Finally, there is the *appeal.* An appeal urges an immediate decision, action, or obedience. Certainly every preacher should preach at least one sermon per week that is followed with an appeal to people to

decide for Christ. Even when people make such decisions in their hearts during a service or alone at home,
there should be a public confession of Christ. An altar
call is a proper conclusion,
and, when one is given,
there need be no other conclusion between the sermon
and the appeal. A decision
call is more effective when it
is given before the hearer
anticipates it. As soon as
people are warned that the
sermon is about to con-
clude, their thoughts wander
to other things, and some
begin to prepare to leave.

Unbelievers

can tell in a minute

whether

the preacher's sermon

is a professional task

or the outgrowth

of a burdened heart.

There is no reason to say that a point or story is the last
unless the speaker wishes to assure the hearers that the
tribulation is nearly over. Let the sermon be of reasonable length, and omit any anticipatory references to the
end. Then let the appeal follow the final point of the
body without a break.

Chapter Ten

Improving Your Preaching Style

A sermon's "style" refers to the distinctive or characteristic mode of construction and presentation.

In works of fine art, there is a characteristic quality that identifies a work as the product of a certain artist. This distinctive quality is called style. Some writers classify several kinds of style, but as there are about as many kinds of style as there are preachers, we will confine our discussion to the necessary qualities of style by which preaching is improved.

How a sermon is constructed in its outline is important, but a well constructed outline is not the sole aim of homiletical studies. How a preacher expresses ideas is practically as important as the construction of an outline. For a sermon to be of highest quality, it should be *clear, precise, beautiful, forceful,* and *interesting.*

> **1. First of all, a sermon must be *clear.*** More than any other people, preachers are obligated to express themselves clearly. After all, the principal task of preaching is to explain to dying men the way of life. Clearness of expression depends upon clear thinking. Preachers may be vague when they try to treat subjects they do not comprehend. A preacher should meditate upon his material, for meditation gives the sermon not only

clarity but also inspiration and originality. An hour of meditation is more fruitful than two hours of reading commentaries, though reading is helpful. Clarity may be advanced by putting thoughts down in writing, though this author does not recommend reading sermons in the pulpit. Clearness is further achieved by the use of simple, non-technical language. It is good to study theology, but the technical language of theology should mostly be kept out of the pulpit. It would be good for preachers to study "The New Testament in Basic English," a translation of the New Testament with a vocabulary of less than one thousand words. Another good book to read often is Bunyan's *The Pilgrim's Progress*.

For preachers, above all people, must be clear in their meaning.

2. A sermon should also be *precise*. Precision is highly dependent upon outline, but most important is the right choice of words. Words should be used that express exactly the thought. No doubt the sermon that is in the preacher's heart and mind is often much better than the sermon that the audience hears, and this difference is often due to a careless choice of words. Every preacher should own and use a good dictionary and thesaurus.

3. A sermon should be *beautiful*. A sermon is not simply a thing to be admired, but as long as beauty of style does not hinder earnestness and sincerity, there is no reason it should be despised. Some of the most beautiful language to be found was uttered by the prophets of the Old Testament and by Jesus in His Sermon on the Mount. An affected style is surely to be avoided, but there is no reason that preachers cannot achieve a beautiful mode of expression that is perfectly natural. One way of achieving an elegant style is the use of figurative language. The discourses of Jesus are filled with figures of speech, especially metaphors and similes. "I am the Light of the world"; I am the Good Shepherd"; "I am the True Vine" are metaphors. "As Moses lifted up the serpent in the wilderness, so must the Son of Man be lifted up" is a simile. "Consider the lilies of the field" is part of a comparison. The analogy, which has already been described, is a figure that aids the achievement of beauty. A constant study of the English Bible is a splendid way to develop beauty of style. Another method to enhance beauty as well as vividness is dramatization, in which the preacher enters into the story and represents one or more of the characters. The imagination must be developed in order for a person to become adept at dramatization. Meditation aids imagination and is necessary not only to clearness but also to beauty. Preachers will find much profit in studying sermons by writers who are known for their beauty of style.

Nothing is more fatal to effective speaking than monotony of tone or pitch.

4. A sermon should be *forceful*. Something in the very nature of the gospel calls for forcefulness of style in its presentation. The gospel message is the most urgent of all messages; its eternal consequences are life and death. The gospel warns of sin's deception and promises incomparable benefits in the transcendent Christ who must be embraced, if ever, within the limits of a fleeting life that is little more than a watch in the night. The purpose of the gospel is to set men free from the bonds of a desperate enemy who knows no scruples in his war against God and righteousness. Furthermore, the gospel offers in Christ the greatest known transforming power for men and nations. It is not strange that Paul said, "Now then, we are ambassadors for Christ, as though God were pleading through us: we implore you on Christ's behalf, be reconciled to God" (2 Corinthians 5:20).

A few well-performed gestures are better than incessant gyrations.

Forceful style requires strong thinking and feeling; it is often enhanced by personal spiritual power and a passion for unsaved people. Forcefulness is sometimes achieved by the use of argument in a sermon. Along with this, there should be rapid movement from point to point. Preachers may find that the Old Testament prophetic books are a good resource for cultivating an energetic style.

5. Finally, a sermon must be *interesting*. In order for a sermon to be interesting, it must have a theme in which people are interested. Except in the classroom, people are little interested in academic or abstract theological matters; they are interested in finding help for their needs, problems, and daily lives. Dramatization, vivid description, figurative language, and apt illustration all aid in the achievement of an interesting style. Another factor in interest is freshness or originality, for people are bored by material that they have heard over and over again. Interest is aided by humor, for we all love to laugh at human blunders. But humor can be easily overdone in a serious sermon, especially near the climax. The best humor is unpremeditated because stale jokes backfire, and humor of questionable propriety ought never to come from the pulpit. Interest is further supported by sympathy. People will naturally be interested in a preacher's sermon when the preacher shows interest in them. Sermons were made for people, not people for sermons. Not least among the aids to sermon interest is action. Appropriate action in the pulpit is good cure for sleepy listeners. Action enhances interest, but preachers must remember "pulpit pounding" can never fully compensate for lack of material. To recapitulate, the interesting sermon has interesting material, vividness, freshness, humor, sympathy, and action.

Artists, sculptors, and musicians spend hours perfecting their techniques and styles in order that their productions may be pleasing and effective aids to finer living. But preachers have the highest of callings and noblest of arts. Their work is done to alter the human will and to transform the character, which must be accomplished, of course, with the aid of God's Spirit. Since they are partnering with God, preachers should view this task as worthy of all the cultivation and perfection that it can be given. There is no reason most preachers cannot increase their congregations and enhance their influence by giving continual attention to the improvement of preaching style.

There is no reason most preachers cannot increase their congregations and enhance their influence by giving continual attention to the improvement of preaching.

What is worth doing for God is worth doing well. If man's part of preaching were only a hundredth part, that little fraction would merit all the years of cultivation a preacher could give it. God defeated the Midianites with only three hundred of Gideon's men, but they were the best three hundred in the nation. If my preaching has only an infinitesimal part to play in the results that follow, I will believe that the Master wants me to do that part with the greatest skill possible; only let me give the Master all the glory, for "I am what I am by the grace of God."

Chapter Eleven

Improving Your Delivery

It is not enough to have a perfect sermon on paper...

For a sermon to achieve its purpose, it must be well delivered. Many sermons that have cost hours of labor and that have been constructed with great care have proved very disappointing because of poor delivery. Even the Bible can be read so that it seems either like dry history or living truth. There are two aspects of delivery—the *physical aspect* and the *spiritual aspect*.

The Physical Aspect of Delivery

1. Bearing and Poise. It is not possible to state exactly how preachers must stand (or sit, if that is the preference), but their posture ought to convey respect for both their calling and their hearers. Poise is a desirable quality, for it puts the audience at ease. A preacher ought to appear completely oriented to his task. If he is awkward, uneasy, or stiff, the hearers also will be uneasy for his sake. While the preacher's posture must have erectness and poise, it must

> *Many sermons that have cost hours of labor and that have been constructed with great care have proved very disappointing because of poor delivery.*

at the same time have freedom. It is not meant that correct posture is bound to any staid patterns; the exact traits will differ from person to person to fit each individual personality.

2. Gestures. As with posture, there are few fixed rules for gestures. However, there is one primary rule: be natural. Awkward and meaningless gestures are to be avoided; gestures are of value only when they are used to give greater force to emphatic words or phrases and when they are synchronized with the emphatic utterances. Nothing is emphatic that is continuous. A few well-performed gestures are better than incessant gyrations. It is best that gestures be spontaneous. Practiced gestures nearly always seem artificial, and the preacher's mind ought to be entirely upon his message, not upon physical details of delivery. Posture and gestures must come to be natural so that they require no attention whatsoever.

> *"Pulpit pounding" can never fully compensate for lack of material.*

3. Voice. The voice is the preacher's most valuable instrument of delivery. Voice makes as much difference in speakers as it does in singers. A trained singer can hold an audience for hours. Spurgeon, who preached to vast audiences before the days of public address systems, owed much of his success to his bell-like penetrating voice. Preachers should take at least enough vocal training to achieve proper voice quality for speaking. There are at least five vocal qualities that a speaker ought to strive for diligently: volume, flexibility, resonance, clear pronunciation, and expression.

The preacher needs **volume,** not in order to thunder during an entire sermon but in order to be heard throughout the whole audience with distinctness and with enough reserve power to lift the voice for emphasis. A car has reserve power in order to ensure an effortless cruising speed, not so that it can be driven at maximum speed all the time. Likewise, speakers should not use their voices at full volume all the time; uniform loudness does not impress people, nor is it a sign of anointing. Even God has a still, small voice. Isaiah said of Jesus, "He will not cry out, nor raise His voice, nor cause His voice to be heard in the street" (Isaiah 42:2). Yet Jesus spoke with anointing and great effectiveness. The best rule is this: Speak in a conversational tone on the average, with enough volume to be easily heard by all, and save the very loud tones for an occasional emphasis. The emphatic voice should be used more frequently at the climax.

Another desirable quality of voice is **flexibility**, or the ability to use a variety of pitches and degrees of volume. Nothing is more fatal to effective speaking than monotony of tone or pitch. Variation is more difficult to achieve when people are nervous, so the first step toward flexibility is relaxation. Then it is good to give attention to varying voice up and down in pitch while speaking, being careful not to develop a sing-song rhythm. Speakers should practice alone occasionally and then engage the aid of a helpful friend who will tell the truth about the vocal faults. It is helpful, too, to listen carefully to good speakers, especially announcers. Singing is another good exercise for achieving a flexible voice.

Something in the very nature of the gospel calls for forcefulness of style in its presentation.

Resonance is a highly desirable attribute for any voice—although this quality is a little more difficult to achieve than the others. It is best cultivated by a short course of vocal training. Resonance is a characteristic of good singing. It is due to the proper combination of tone and overtones. Resonance depends upon the proper placement of the voice and the use of the diaphragm. A resonant voice will have greater carrying power and will enable a speaker to be heard farther with less volume. Speakers may use full volume and not be heard distinctly even in small buildings if their voice quality is poor. But the greatest value of resonance is that it gives the voice a musical quality that is very pleasant to hear.

Too much cannot be said for the need of **clear pronunciation**. Americans have a habit of running words together; some preachers speak unclearly yet expect people to listen patiently. The best exercise to overcome poor pronunciation is careful reading aloud in the presence of a helpful friend and critic. Special attention should be given to pronouncing initial and final consonants. Preachers should not speak so rapidly that they cannot carefully pronounce words for there is a tendency in many buildings with imperfect acoustics for words to run together.

Good expression is a much needed vocal quality for preaching. A sentence may mean several things or nothing, depending upon the inflection of the voice. A sentence may appear to be either a weak apology or a confident defense; the difference is the expression put into its utterance. The voice is capable of expressing love, anger, sympathy, joy, sorrow, censure, or approval in its very tones apart from the content of the message. There is no reason preachers should not cultivate the ability to put full meaning into what they say, for preachers, above all people, must be clear in their meaning. Many people have been offended because the tone of voice seemed to say something other than what the speaker meant. But the greatest

It is good to study theology, but the technical language of theology should mostly be kept out of the pulpit.

value of expression is its power to clothe words with life and fullness of meaning so that people may be moved to action.

The Spiritual Aspect of Delivery

Delivery, of course, as applied to preaching, is not entirely a matter of elocution. There are spiritual qualities of speaking and action that are positively vital to gospel preaching. Four of these will be treated here: *burden, anointing, zeal, and faith.*

Even a deep sermon must be crystal clear in the conclusion, or it can have no practical success.

1. **In addition to a genuine Christian experience and Holy Spirit empowerment for service, preachers need a sincere burden for lost and needy souls.** Unbelievers can tell in a minute whether the preacher's sermon is a professional task or the outgrowth of a burdened heart. Preachers must read their Bibles enough and pray enough to be genuinely moved with love and passion for lost souls. To love people, we must contact people. Preachers cannot spend all their time in their studies and develop or maintain a true concern for unsaved people. They must visit the needy, become acquainted with their respective communities and their problems, and do active personal evangelism if they are to maintain a passion for souls.

2. **Nothing is more needed in preaching than anointing.** But no quality is more misunderstood. Anointing is not loudness or rapidity of speech. It is not the tone of voice, the gestures or, in fact, any physical thing. The anointing is a spiritual force of conviction that God puts into a preacher's message that causes it to bring results. Anointing is not the gift of automatic utterance

that makes it unnecessary for a preacher to study or prepare a sermon. The sermon is the preacher's task; the anointing is God's work, and no sermon can ever bring permanent spiritual results without God's anointing. Anointing in the Old Testament was a symbol of the divine authority that was vested in a leader. The anointing is God's seal of authority upon a sermon that makes it speak to the hearts of hearers. Anointing is obtained by prayer and complete reliance upon God for the results of the sermon, but it is not inconsistent with careful study, meditation, and personal development.

A proposition can be more successfully enforced if the hearers have first been shown what the proposition means and that it is reasonable and scriptural.

3. **Among the spiritual aspects of delivery is zeal, or earnestness.** True religious zeal is a product of spirituality and is rarely possessed by a worldly person of carnal interests or a mere professional preacher. Zealous people are convinced that they are doing the most important and most needed work in the world. Let no one contemplate entering the ministry who is not sincerely convinced that preaching the gospel is the most vital and urgent of all callings. Prayer is the best exercise for achieving zeal.

4. **In addition to burden, anointing, and zeal, faith is a valuable and necessary spiritual quality of delivery.** Preachers must believe that God is going to honor His Word and accomplish the purpose of the sermon. A sermon's effect is greatly hindered the very moment

that doubt creeps into the preacher's heart about God's ability or willingness to give the sermon success.

Many successful evangelists say that they can visualize full altars while they are preaching their sermons. A noted evangelist was asked, "How do you win so many converts?" He responded: "I ask God to help me; then I believe with all my heart that souls will accept Christ, and they always do." God is still saving souls where His Word is preached powerfully. If we ask God for results, seek results, and believe in results, all Satan's hosts cannot stop the advance of the gospel.

Chapter Twelve

Preparing a Sermon Series

There are a great many things that could be said...

...for the importance of preaching in series. Briefly, these are the main advantages:

1. Some subjects are too big to be handled adequately in one sermon. It is much better to divide the subject into two or three parts and do justice to each than to make one sermon too long, yet still incomplete.

2. Christian duties that church members are prone to neglect can seldom be enforced in a single sermon. It often requires a series of several such sermons before sufficient conviction is created to stir all the negligent members to activity. For instance, it will usually require several sermons on personal evangelism before people will systematically begin to witness for Christ.

A good introduction will contain a clear statement of the theme and purpose of the sermon.

3. In order for people to have whole views of Bible doctrines or Bible books, it is necessary to study consecutively the parts in their relationship. The subjects

treated in many churches are so unrelated and disconnected that people have no chance to obtain an organized picture of any doctrine or book.

**4. People's interest is sustained if the series is not
continued too long.** If the first sermon in a series is
interesting, the hearers will want to be present for all
the following sermons.

Types of Series

**1. The most common type of sermon series is the
topical series.** This consists of two or more aspects or
phases of a topic or several related topics. The following illustrates a series of phases of one subject:

I.   The Need for Personal Evangelism
II. Our Bible Examples in Personal Evangelism
III. The Best Methods of Personal Evangelism

A series on the work of Christ could include the follow-
ing:
- Propitiation
- Redemption
- Reconciliation
- Justification
- Sanctification

These one-word subjects could be lengthened a bit, but
it would hardly be practical to give illustrations here
because different people and different communities
would be appealed to differently. Topics that attract in
one place repel in another.

**2. Next there is the *biographical* series, which consists
of treating related deeds, characteristics, or periods**

of one Bible character or of related Bible characters.
The life of Moses may be divided into three periods of
forty years each:

    I.   The Young Hero and His Great Blunders
    II. The Obscure Shepherd and His Great Call
    III. The Successful Leader and His Great Patience

A series on related characters might be on the patri-
archs Abraham, Isaac, Jacob, and Joseph, with a sermon
on each. Likewise, a series could be developed on the
good kings of Judah or the twelve disciples.

**3. Especially good for teaching and easily adaptable
for preaching is the series on a *book of the Bible.*** In
this type of series, a book of the Bible may be considered chapter-by-chapter. Also, many preachers prefer to
use the paragraph as a unit, taking only the highlight-
ed portions and omitting the portions in between that
are not quite so relevant to the purpose of the series.
The paragraph is a better natural division than a chapter in most cases. With a long book, however, a paragraph series could become tiresome. It may be very
practical to prepare a series on related books such as
the Minor Prophets or the Pastoral Epistles. A series on
Philippians could be very inspiring and profitable;
treated by chapters, it would require four weeks, which
is about right for the average series. Consider the following outline of a series on Philippians:

    I.   Christ, the Believer's Life—Chapter 1
    II. Christ, the Believer's Example—Chapter 2
    III. Christ, the Believer's Goal—Chapter 3
    IV. Christ, the Believer's Peace—Chapter 4

Many pastors find it profitable to precede Easter with a series on one of the Synoptic Gospels so that the Palm Sunday and Resurrection accounts match the days on the Christian calendar. What better way could there be of acquainting people with the life of Christ and of appropriately approaching Easter season! The incidents and discourses of the life of Christ provide opportunity for discussing most all of the needs and problems of the Christian life and service. Further, they provide unparalleled opportunity to lift up Christ, which is the supreme objective of the Christian ministry. It will probably be better to treat the long Gospels by considering only the salient passages in order not to extend the series too long. Mark's Gospel is best to begin with because it is the shortest and the most vivid. The following list of topics, for instance, could be used in an extended series on the book of Mark:

The prelude to the sermon should have only one idea.

The Mighty Forerunner	Mark 1:2-8
The Ministry of Healing	Mark 2:12
The Question of the Sabbath	Mark 2:23–3:6
The True Relatives of Christ	Mark 3:20-35
Sowing Gospel Seed	Mark 4:1-20
From the Tombs to the Ministry	Mark 5:1-20
The Faith of a Foreigner	Mark 7:24-30
Conditions of Discipleship	Mark 8:33-38
The Real Glory of God's Son	Mark 9:1-8
The Man who Lacked One Thing	Mark 10:17-27
His Majesty, the King!	Mark 11:1-11
A Poor Widow's Mighty Gift	Mark 12:41-44
The Blood Covenant	Mark 14:18-26
Ashamed of Jesus	Mark 14:66-72

The Cross against the Sky	Mark 15:21-41
Victory over Death	Mark 16:1-8
Signs Following	Mark 16:15-20

Preparing a Series

A series should never be announced until the book has been thoroughly studied in advance and all the individual sermons have been at least worked out in outline form. Otherwise, a series that appears attractive may be very difficult or inappropriate, and the pastor may be tempted to discontinue the series midway through. In the case of a topical series, a preacher may discover that there is not material available for good sermons on all the subjects announced. So it is best never to announce a series until it has been carefully prepared. If a preacher just once fails to complete a series, any others that are announced later will attract no attention. It is best not to announce the number of sermons at the beginning of the series.

A series, like an individual sermon, should be selected to coincide with the needs or interests of the people. It is good to arrange the series, if possible, so that it fits the season of the year. Book series are most applicable preceding Easter and in the fall months of the year. Topical series should arise out of a desire to meet certain needs or problems of the people. Where unforeseen problems arise during a series, the series can be interrupted with a special sermon; the preacher can return to the series afterward.

Difficult concepts can be made clear if they are built on a lucid foundation and approached systematically.

It is not good to have more than one series going at the same time. One service should be reserved for the occasional type sermon so that special needs may be met as they arise. While the whole series must be carefully planned and studied in advance, the final preparation of the individual sermons should be left for the week of preaching. Series preaching certainly has many arguments in its favor, and every preacher should occasionally try it; it will prove a blessing to the preacher as well as to the hearers.

Chapter Thirteen

Preaching to Persuade

Preaching is the oral communication of divine truth with a view to persuasion.

Preaching is not mere communication; it always has a goal to motivate hearers to make a decision and to take some form of action. While it is true that the strongest persuasive force is the work of the Holy Spirit, it is also true that human instruments are involved in properly motivating men. Paul said, "Knowing, therefore, the terror of the Lord, we persuade men" (2 Corinthians 5:11).

Most people have an aversion to abruptness, and are not ready to concentrate on an idea without preparation.

Describing Paul's planting of the church at Ephesus, Luke writes: "And he went into the synagogue and spoke boldly for three months, reasoning and persuading concerning the things of the kingdom of God." (Acts 19:8). In this chapter, I would like to point out some of the factors that contribute to persuasive preaching.

Character and Good Example

Writing to the Thessalonian church, the apostle Paul reminded them, "We are well pleased to impart to you, not only the gospel of God, but also our own lives" (1 Thessalonians 2:8). There is no doubt that a preacher's character and quality of life can strongly reinforce his reasoning about righteousness.

The majority of preachers are people of character and sound spirituality. Those few who lack godliness, however, or have compromised Christian morality—even though their misdeeds are concealed—find their preaching wanting persuasion. When the Apostolic Church was looking for seven men to carry out a special task, they sought "men of good reputation, full of the Holy Spirit and wisdom."

> *A sermon without a skeleton is like a man without a backbone. But just as a man must be more than bones, so must a sermon be more than skeleton. The skeleton must be clothed with living flesh.*

Stephen was one such man of character. Luke describes him as "full of faith and power," and notes that he "did great wonders and signs among the people." (Acts 6:3,8). Another of these seven was Philip, who performed great miracles in Samaria and who gained a wide audience in the city (Acts 8:6). Both Stephen and Philip were persuasive because they were men of honest and godly report. They were respected for their Christ like character.

A Strong Presence of God and a Spirit of Worship

Preaching is a function of the Church, the Body of Christ. Most preaching is performed as a part of a Christian service of worship. The sermon is not an appendage to worship; it is a part of it. When the church assembles in Christ's Name, He is present in the midst to receive the worship of the saints and to administer grace. Preaching is a function of the ministers placed in Christ's Body to equip the saints. This preaching of gifted pastor-teachers, according to Scripture (1 John 2:20, 27), bears the Spirit's anointing.

In Paul's writing to the Thessalonians, he stated, "For our gospel did not come to you in word only, but also in power, and in the Holy Spirit and in much assurance, as you know what kind of men we were among you for your sake. And you became followers of us and of the Lord." Such preaching was powerfully persuasive for they "turned to God from idols to serve the living and true God" (1 Thessalonians 1:5, 6, 9).

The Apostle often urged saints to pray for him that he might preach as he ought to preach (Ephesians 6:18-20). A prayerful, worshiping church can greatly help their pastor to be a persuasive preacher.

Well Organized Sermons

A well organized sermon is not only easier to follow and easier to remember but often more persuasive as well. It stands to reason that a sermon with points and arguments that are easier to grasp and to retain will have a

A sermon without a strong theme is like a flood that spreads in every direction; a sermon with a theme is like a river flowing within its banks in a certain direction.

greater effect on the hearer than one that is unclear and difficult to follow. It also makes sense that a sermon that makes the message of a Scripture passage clear and easy to apply will be a more effective sermon than the one that fails to follow a straight course.

This fact is brought out forcefully in a passage from the book of Nehemiah: "And the Levites, helped the people to understand the Law…. So they read distinctly from the book, in the Law of God; and they gave the sense, and helped them to understand the reading. And all the people went their way to eat and drink, to send portions and rejoice greatly, because they understood the words that were declared to them (Nehemiah 8:7-8, 12).

The expository sermon need not be delivered in the calm tone of the classroom; it can be and should be forceful and impassioned.

Here is true expository preaching. It was powerful in the motivational effect upon the people. If we can make the Scriptures clear, understandable, and memorable, our preaching will accomplish more nearly its divinely intended purpose of changing lives.

A part of good organization is to have a good introduction and conclusion. A good introduction is needed because people may not listen attentively unless their interest is aroused at the beginning. A sermon should be introduced in a way sufficiently striking as to gain attention and make the hearers wish to hear the sermon through to the end. Further, a sermon must have a strong conclusion that motivates to some specific decision or action. No one is ever persuaded toward an undefined goal.

Enthusiasm

Paul wrote to Titus about zeal, saying this concerning the Lord Jesus: "Who gave Himself for us, that He might redeem us from every lawless deed and purify for Himself His own special people, zealous for good works" (Titus 2:14). To the Galatians he said, "But it is good to be zealous in a good thing always, and not only when I am present with you" (Galatians 4:18).

Nothing is clearer than that the great Apostle Paul exercised his ministry with great enthusiasm. At the end of his ministry, even as a prisoner, he preached Jesus with enthusiasm, "per-

suading them concerning Jesus" (Acts 28:23). He preach,
a hardhearted audience, but in spite of it, some believed. The,
were persuaded by his zealous and enthusiastic reasoning.

Sales people will have little success trying to sell products
about which they are apathetic. We, too, must, by prayer and
devotion, maintain a love for the Word, a passion for souls,
and an enthusiasm for our ministry if our preaching is to be
persuasive.

In our day, we see a tendency for preachers to strive for a
casualness in the pulpit. No, one doesn't have to shout his sermon nor pound the pulpit, but the message we preach is of
such import that, if we ourselves feel its great potential, we cannot but present it with a discernable enthusiasm.

Relevance to Today's Needs

A criticism sometimes leveled against expository preaching
is that it sets forth endless details about people and situations
of ancient history, but lacks application
to the needs of our day. In some cases,
this criticism may be valid, but it is not
true of general expository preaching.

All Bible preaching done properly is
more than a lecture; it strives for decisions and actions. In fact, the Bible,
being God's inspired Word for all ages of
time, is as relevant today as it was when
first penned. We do strive to get at the
original intent of a passage as it was
directed to the particular recipients, but
we then derive a spiritual principle that
speaks to modern believers with contemporary problems. When we show

*Preaching
is a true part
of the church's
worship.
In fact,
it may be the
crowning event
in the
worship service.*

that the Bible message is timeless and that it speaks powerfully
to current situations, we preach it persuasively. When people
today with guilt, bereavement, sorrow, temptation, anxiety, envy,

fear, shame, frustration, pain, and affliction are shown that the Bible has a word of healing and redemption for each problem, they receive that message gladly.

To preach persuasively, we start with a foundation of godly character. We then empower the message with the presence of the Holy Spirit in an atmosphere of worship. With that under-girding, we give the message a clear, organized structure, aim it to contemporary needs, and deliver it with enthusiasm. With the Spirit's anointing and the preacher's diligence, the message has the potential to transform situations and men.

Selected Bibliography

Beecher, Lyman. *Lectures on Preaching at Yale.* New York: Dodd-Mead, 1896.

Black, James MacDougall. *The Mystery of Preaching.* Chicago: Revell, 1935.

Blackwood, Arthur Watterson. *Fine Art of Preaching.* New York: MacMillan, 1937.

_____. *Planning a Year's Pulpit Work.* New York: Abingdon-Cokesbury, 1942.

_____. *Preaching From the Bible.* New York: Abingdon-Cokesbury, 1941.

Broadus, John Albert. *Treatise on the Preparation and Delivery of Sermons.* Philadelphia: Smith, English & Co., 1870.

Brooks, Phillips. *Lectures on Preaching.* New York, Dutton, 1902.

Bryan, Dawson Charles. *The Art of Illustrating Sermons.* Nashville: Cokesbury, 1938.

Burrell, David James. *The Sermon, Its Construction and Delivery.* New York: Revell, 1913.

Dale, Robert William. *Nine Lectures on Preaching.* New York: A.S. Barnes, 1878.

Evans, William. *How to Prepare Sermons and Gospel Addresses.* Chicago: Bible Institute Colportage, 1913.

Fisk, Franklin. *Manual of Preaching.* Los Angeles: Armstrong, 1895.

Hoyt, Arthur Stephen. *The Preacher.* New York: MacMillan, 1909.

_____. *Vital Elements of Preaching.* New York: MacMillan, 1914.

_____. *Work of Preaching.* New York: MacMillan, 1927.

Johnson, Herrick. *The Ideal Ministry.* New York: Revell, 1908.

Jowett, John Henry. *The Preacher, His Life and Work.* New York: Hodder & Stoughton, 1912.

Kern, John Adam. *The Ministry to the Congregation.* New York: Ketcham, 1897.

Kidder, Daniel Parish. *A Treatise on Homiletics*. New York: Carlton & Porter, 1864.

Knott, Harold Elkin. *How to Prepare an Expository Sermon*. Cincinnati: Standard Publishing, 1930.

Lenski, Richard C.H. *The Sermon, Its Homiletical Construction*. Columbus: Lutheran Book Concern, 1866.

Montgomery, James Alan. *Preparing Preachers to Preach*. Grand Rapids:Zondervan Publishing House, 1939.

Oman, John Wood. *Concerning the Ministry*. Richmond: John Knox, 1963.

Pattison, Thomas Harwood. *The Making of a Sermon*. Philadelphia: American Baptist Publication Society, 1900.

Phelps, Austin. *The Theory of Preaching*. New York: Scribner's, 1881.

Pierson, Arthur Tappan. *Knowing the Scriptures*. New York: Gospel Publishing 1910.

Ray, Jefferson Davis. *Expository Preaching*. Grand Rapids: Zondervan, 1940.

Thomas, William. *Ministerial Life and Work*. Chicago: Bible Institute Colportage, 1927.